The Wealthy Paper Carriers

WHAT STUDENTS SAY ABOUT "THE WEALTHY PAPER CARRIERS"...

"An excellent book that's fun to read yet very useful. I enjoyed how it gave real life experiences instead of just telling you what to do."

Sarah Mc Ateer, Age 11

"This book contains 'common-cents' advice for bewildered young adults. Sit down with Uncle Bill...guru of Money Management and find out all you wanted to know about...growing up financially."

Andy Leung, Age 16

"A wonderful introduction to the Canadian financial scene. Great for young people to explore monetary independence."

Melanie Justason, Age 17

AND HOW THE REVIEWERS REACTED...

"Zimmer tries to show teens they have time on their sides, urging them to use whatever skills and hobbies they've got to develop business opportunities."

Chris Dawson, Calgary Herald

"I wish this book had been around when I was young. The ideas and advice are what every parent would want their children to know."

Chris Curtis, Entrepreneurship Consultant
Nova Scotia Department of Education

THE SPRINGBANK
WEALTHY SERIES

"I'm proud of this book because I believe it to be a much-needed guide to the competitive world of the Nineties. Written in the form of an entertaining story, it shows how—by following a few simple principles—young adults can aspire to more in life than servile jobs with no prestige and no future. It demonstrates that success is more a matter of working *intelligently* than excessively.

"I have written the book in fictional style to make the idea of financial planning less intimidating, and I've enlisted the help of the inimitable Ben Wicks to emphasize some salient points.

"My intent is quite simple. Without patronizing humbug or business jargon, I show how you can set goals and priorities and I demonstrate how to achieve them through simple step-by-step planning. The book reflects my personal belief that continuing self-improvement is not only necessary for life satisfaction but is essential to human survival .

"I hope you enjoy reading *The Wealthy Paper Carriers* as much as I enjoyed writing it."

Henry B. Zimmer

THE WEALTHY PAPER CARRIERS

A STORY OF FINANCIAL MOTIVATION
FOR YOUNG ADULTS

HENRY B. CIMMER

SPRINGBANK PUBLISHING

Published in 1993 by
Springbank Publishing
5425 Elbow Drive SW
Calgary, Alberta
T2V 1H7

First printing October 1993

Canadian Cataloguing in Publication Data
Cimmer, Henry B., 1943-
The Wealthy Paper Carriers

ISBN 1-895653-09-6

1. Youth–Finance, Personal 2. Young adults–
Finance, Personal. 3. Savings and thrift. I. Title.
HG179.C544 1993 332.024'055 C93-091864-9

Design: Rocket Science Design Limited

Printed and bound in Canada

ACKNOWLEGEMENTS

I am indebted to a number of people for their help in creating this book. Most particularly, I acknowledge the assistance of Helen Siemens and her spring 1993 Career and Life Management class at Lester B. Pearson High School in Calgary. Their input was invaluable.

I am especially grateful to the students who helped me by reading the draft manuscript and improving it through their constructive comments. They include: Melanie Justason, Andy Leung, and Sarah and Catherine McAteer.

Special thanks go to Dr. Sharon Gibb—for demonstrating how educational systems operate and for showing me how to write the book in a manner appropriate for inclusion in school curricula.

It is my good fortune to work with a number of talented people, all of whom deserve mention. My thanks to Sue Blanchard, my partner in Springbank Publishing, for her unflagging encouragement and support. Appreciation also goes to the production team: to Denton and Harold Pendergast for the cover and book design; to Sherry Willetts and Janet King for keyboarding many, many drafts; and to eagle-eyed proofreader Linda Jarrett.

Kathy Blood provided sound advice throughout and Carol Hutchins lent her considerable expertise to the sections of the book concerned with the purchase of real estate.

Thanks also to John Newton for his inspired contributions to the production of advertising and promotional materials.

CONTENTS

CHAPTER ONE

DECEMBER 6, 2015
LOGAN'S STORY: LOOKING BACK

DON'T YOU EVER WISH you could get hold of the guy who invented birthdays and punch him or her right in the nose? Finding birthday presents is tough at the best of times—but what do you get for the man who's got everything? In this case it's our Uncle Bill who turns 65 next week.

My name is Logan Lavery and I'm.... Oh well, you'll find out soon enough. Anyway, my sister Andrea and I never really knew our Uncle Bill before we were teenagers. But in these last 20 years, he's been more than just a relative. He's become our friend and mentor. It's a tough world out there once you leave school and go out and try to make something of yourself. Without our Uncle Bill we probably would have floundered like so many of our peers.

It was Uncle Bill who taught us it's no sin to become wealthy and you don't have to be a villainous opportunist who knifes the little guy in the back to make it to the top. He showed us how we could set goals, make plans and follow them. He never knocked the school system (as it then was) but gently and subtly convinced us there was more to education than what we could get out of a classroom. Fortunately, things have changed in the last 20 years—for the better, I might add. Yet those were unsettled times 20 years ago when Andrea and I were in Grade 11.

We're not twins, although many people assume we are. And when I write about being in Grade 11 at the same time I'm proud to say neither of us ever failed. Actually, Andrea was born in early January 1980 and I came along just a little over 11 months later on December 3. I guess Mom and Dad must have figured their

1

bedroom activities would be "safe" for a while right after Andrea was born, but somebody up there must've had a good time playing tricks on them. Anyway, after I was born, they probably started doing things a little bit differently because there's just the two of us.

More to the point, though, because of school age-cutoffs, we wound up in the same grade. In the early years, the schools sometimes tried to put us into different classes. But we really functioned quite well together and after a bit of intervention from Mom, sometime around Grade 3 or 4, the powers that were decided it would be okay for us to do our schooling together.

I'd be lying if I tried to tell you we always did our homework independently. In fact, it was quite convenient to be able to split math assignments and each do only half the questions. In our defence, though, we did tackle *major* projects on our own, and sometimes even made a concerted effort to choose different topics to research and write about. But I guess I'm rambling a bit. So I'll try to get back on track and tell the story of Uncle Bill and how he so greatly affected our lives.

Andrea and I got together for dinner the other night with our families as we usually do two or three times a month and we started to talk about an appropriate birthday present for him. We decided the best present we could give Uncle Bill would be to tell our story. When it's all down on paper, we're sure he'll enjoy reading it and re-living these last two decades. We hope that some time in the next few years, our kids will enjoy it too. I've got two of my own and Andrea is expecting her first. Better late than never.

I mentioned that Uncle Bill's birthday is next week and here we are just starting to write this book. You might be wondering how we're ever going to have it finished in time. Well, thank God for the latest technology. For my birthday, my wife, Colleen, got me one of these new computers with Pro-Edit 5.1 software. Colleen is an interior designer who specializes in custom home design using virtual reality technology. She sits down at her computer with her clients and, in a matter of a few hours, she can have a whole house designed to meet almost any taste or budget. It's all quite amazing, but she knows the stuff backwards, forwards, and sideways.

Anyhow, about my new computer—anybody can use it. All you have to do is talk to it. You don't even have to punch keys any more, and with the Pro-Edit feature, you don't even have to worry about grammar, punctuation or (believe it or not) sentence structure! This baby can take a bunch of semi-garbled thoughts and put them into language that any professional writer would envy. In fact, Colleen told me the next version of Pro-Edit will actually enable the user to pick one of 35 styles taken from those used by current best-selling authors! So, if you have a story to tell and select an old master like Stephen King from the menu, bingo, even the experts won't be able to tell whether you wrote it or he did. Colleen said the Writer's Guild is trying to suppress this feature and is threatening plagiarism action but I guess you can't stop progress. I know it's a little hard to explain, but as I see these pages coming out of my printer, I ask myself whether I really wrote this! Not bad for someone who hasn't taken an English course in over 20 years. It sure would have been nice to have a computer like this unit and this latest software when I was going to school. Kids today sure have it easier than Andrea and I did back when we had to do all our *own* thinking, let alone our own typing.

Enough of these digressions. Even with all the technical assistance, if I don't get down to business, we'll never finish in time for Uncle Bill's party. Besides, Andrea is sitting right here just itching to take over so I'd better get some of this background out of the way.

❧

It all started in 1995, when our Uncle Bill moved to Ottawa from Calgary. As Charles Dickens once said, "It was the best of times; it was the worst of times." The government was spending fortunes trying to convince us the long drawn out recession of the early '90s had ended. But there weren't a whole lot of jobs out there and even at age 15 or 16 in Grade 11, many of us were starting to get nervous. Not a week went by but someone would come in all crest-fallen and angry, telling us that his or her mom or dad had just gotten notice. I'll never forget the day when Corey Lavoie, who was one of my closest friends at the time, announced sorrowfully that he would have to quit the basketball team in order to take a job bagging groceries after school because his dad's unemployment benefits had run out.

A lot of us were coming to the conclusion that we could very well be part of the first generation that wouldn't have things better than our parents. Our teacher in our health and lifestyles course had brought in a copy of a book called *"Generation X"* which Andrea and I thought was one of the most depressing tales imaginable. It was about some characters who were born around 1960 who had decided to drop out, rather than work at what the author of *"Generation X"* called "McJobs"—"low-pay, low-prestige, low-benefit, no-future jobs in the service industry". I remember thinking if people in their 20s and 30s felt *they* would be doomed to a life of McJobs, what could my friends and I have to look forward to?

Our teachers weren't a whole lot of help; I suppose because they, themselves, had achieved some reasonable security in *their* lives, many of them felt (somewhat simplistically) that all you really needed to get ahead was a good education, as in the past. They tried to convey the impression that things would automatically fall into place for us, too. We would all eventually get married, have children of our own, a house in the suburbs, two cars, and two cats in the yard. The education system hadn't yet started to evolve the way it would in the next decade. There was still a lack of communication between the sheltered environment of the school system and the cold cruel world. Our teachers didn't emphasize the fact that over 50 per cent of all marriages ended in divorce (and, presumably, a large percentage of those unions that remained were not particularly happy). I remember reading an article that quoted a marriage counsellor in Victoria who said that money squabbles were the biggest marriage wrecker—much more so than sex, alcohol or drug abuse.

Looking back, maybe most of the teachers felt *they* had it made—secure jobs with pensions at the end. It was hard for them to teach us the importance of setting goals, making plans and then following them. It wasn't all their fault—for many reasons, not the least of which was that few of us knew at age 15 what we wanted to do with our own lives. None of us really comprehended how important it would be to maintain flexibility and to recognize that, in all probability, we would have three or four different kinds of jobs or careers in a changing roller-coaster world.

Fortunately, today in the 21st Century, things are quite different and I don't think our kids—Andrea's and mine—will have to go through the same kind of confusion we did. I'm pleased to say today, health and lifestyles courses are considered as important as the old three Rs: reading, 'riting and 'rithmetic. Vocational courses are no longer restricted to those students who are less than academically gifted. The ability to do things with one's hands is now more the "in thing" than the ability to conjure things up in one's head.

Andrea and I were lucky. We had our Uncle Bill to show us the way—to give us direction—at a time when our school hadn't yet evolved to meet the challenges of the 21st Century.

Uncle Bill is Mom's older brother. They grew up in Montreal and lived there until the late 1970s when Rene Levesque came into power and threatened to take Quebec out of Confederation. At that time, a lot of English-speaking people left. Mom and Dad went to Ottawa while Uncle Bill went west to Calgary. Dad was a pharmacist until his premature death five years ago. He was a very quiet man, quite wrapped up in his stores and although he certainly never abused us, Andrea and I really weren't all that close to him. He and Mom seemed to get along pretty well, in spite of the fact that she nagged him quite a bit (and deservedly so) for his tendency to over-eat and his love of junk foods. If he had listened to her, perhaps he never would've had the heart attack that ended his life so tragically. I remember Mom and Dad talking about retirement plans, travel, and so on. It's sad that all their hopes and dreams of fading into the sunset together never did materialize.

Mom got her training as a physiotherapist at McGill and

still works at the Ottawa General three days a week. Recently, she met this radiologist and who knows...? If we ever write a sequel, we'll keep you informed.

So, back to Uncle Bill. Like I said, he was a shadowy character at the time Andrea and I were growing up. Mom told us he was a tax accountant. I can remember Andrea sticking out her tongue and braying the word "b-o-r-i-n-g". There were all these shows on TV about glamorous lawyers, but no one ever made an

IF DONALD TRUMP CALLS, TAKE A NUMBER

WICKS

accountant into a hero. It seems, though, that sometime in the early 1980s our Uncle wrote a book on income taxes which achieved quite a bit of prominence. Over the next few years, he apparently got involved in lecturing on income taxes and financial planning to business groups across Canada. He came to Ottawa once or twice when we were little, although we never did have more than a dinner or two together. As we later learned, Ottawa was not the best place for him at the time because his material was much more geared towards business owners, entrepreneurs and professionals than to civil servants.

Then in the late 1980s, Uncle Bill struck it rich. He developed a computer software program to do income tax returns, and according to Mom, it grew into an enormously successful business. He and Aunt Helen bought a winter home in Phoenix, and to hear Mom tell the story, it seems that every other week they were in some exotic place, down in the Caribbean, Europe or you name it. One afternoon in 1993, Mom called Andrea and me into the kitchen and dropped what she thought was a major bombshell. "Uncle Bill and Aunt Helen are getting divorced," she told us. If truth be told, Andrea and I didn't really care. To be honest, we hardly knew Uncle Bill and Aunt Helen and they weren't all that real. We had never even gotten to know our cousins who at that time were in universities in the west.

Over the next few months, I vaguely recall a few snippets out of my parents' hushed conversations relating to the 'divorce scandal of the century'. Although it seemed that Uncle Bill had offered Aunt Helen a reasonable ongoing monthly income, she wanted a cash settlement so she wouldn't be dependent on his support. To make a long story short, in 1994 Uncle Bill sold his software business and retired at the age of 44. The buyer was a public company listed on the Toronto Stock Exchange and I can remember the sale was even reported in the Ottawa Times-Herald business section. Dad pointed it out to Mom one morning over breakfast and Andrea and I snuck a peek later on. I remember my Dad's expression when he told Mom "your brother won't ever have to work again, lucky devil, even if Helen winds up with quite a big chunk".

After the business was sold, Uncle Bill took a year off to do some travelling and then, right after New Year's 1995, I remember Andrea and I came home from school one day to find our mother smiling in the kitchen.

"Guess what?" she asked.

"What?" we replied.

"Your Uncle Bill has decided to move to Ottawa. I guess he's grown tired of globe-trotting and wants to get a fresh start. He'll be here in two weeks."

It was difficult for us to share Mom's enthusiasm, although being well brought up and polite kids (ahem), Andrea and I made some appropriate comments and then went off to do our own thing.

Two weeks later on a Sunday afternoon, Dad went out to the airport to pick up Uncle Bill and bring him home for dinner. Mom cooked up a storm and made a lemon meringue pie which she told us was always our uncle's favourite. When Dad and Uncle Bill came back carrying a couple of seemingly expensive and yet well-worn suitcases, I can't say we were overly impressed. Uncle Bill was rather tall, standing at just over six feet. He was reasonably slim and sported a bushy black moustache. His hair was still mainly jet black although it was starting to recede a bit at the front. He had warm brown eyes, but there was a certain reserve about him that sort of told us he needed his own space.

The conversation over dinner that night between Uncle Bill and our parents was rather lively, although Andrea and I were pretty well excluded. Uncle Bill told Mom and Dad quite a bit about his travels over the last year but very pointedly stayed away from discussing his marriage breakdown. He indicated he would be buying a condo apartment in downtown Ottawa and expected to do some income tax consulting and writing just to keep busy. Mom asked him where he was staying and he mentioned he had booked a suite at the Chateau Laurier for the following week. At that point, she began to insist that Uncle Bill stay with us (while Dad squirmed a bit in his chair) but Uncle Bill declined firmly, insisting he didn't want to put anyone out. Mom offered to lend him her car for a day or so but he again declined, telling her his car had already arrived by train from Calgary. Eventually, though, Uncle Bill agreed to stay with us for a month or two until his condo was ready for occupancy. Mom was beside herself with joy, although Dad's reaction wasn't nearly as enthusiastic.

If you had asked Andrea or me that night about how *we* felt, I suspect our response would not have been all that favourable. Our routine was being interrupted and although it was clear that Mom loved her brother very much, I think Dad found Uncle Bill a bit intimidating. Not that Uncle Bill did anything to put Dad off, but it seems many people do find it uncomfortable to be around people who are clearly wealthy and successful. Certainly, Andrea and I hadn't a clue about how Uncle Bill would ultimately affect our lives.

So this is our story. It's about Andrea and me and how we both wound up wealthy because of what we learned from our Uncle Bill. In many ways, it's an ordinary story about discipline, planning and sticking to the task at hand while keeping an eye fixed on a goal. If *you* can learn something, benefit from it, and have some fun and a good read along the way, Andrea and I will gain a great sense of accomplishment. Most of all, this is our birthday present to Uncle Bill. What better way for us to thank him?

Chapter Two
February 1995
Andrea's Story: How Our Futures Almost Went Up in Smoke

That afternoon, Lenny Fong had given Logan and me a couple of cigarettes from a pack he had "borrowed" from his father the night before. Logan and I were standing on the patio outside our kitchen puffing away, trying to look cool in spite of the sub-zero temperature. We didn't dare try to savour our forbidden treasure in the house because we were afraid Mom and Dad would smell the smoke when they came home from work an hour or two later.

I remember feeling quite grown up at the time—at least until I started to choke on a puff that seemed to go down the wrong way. Logan started to pound me on the back, laughing uproariously and peppering me with comments like "wimp" and "geek". I was busy gasping for breath and couldn't really respond as I felt the tears freezing on my cheeks.

All at once, we sensed a presence behind us. We turned and there was Uncle Bill. We had completely forgotten he had recently moved from Calgary to Ottawa and he was, for a short time, our house guest. To say the least, we were shocked to see him hovering over us.

"Hi, guys," Uncle Bill said, studiously ignoring the smoldering butts clenched in our icy fingers. "Did you have a good day at school?"

"Wh-what are you doing here?" Logan stammered as he flicked his cigarette into the deep snow.

"For now, I live here," said Uncle Bill, "although you may be pleased to know you won't be burdened with me for too much longer. I've just bought a condo-apartment at the Rideau Towers downtown. I should be moving in next week if I can get my furniture out of storage and then I'll have you guys over. It's got a sauna, hot-tub and pool and I think you just might enjoy them."

I began to relax when I could see Uncle Bill wasn't going to read us the riot act over our little smoking escapade. I suppose Logan and I knew full-well the dangers of prolonged smoking. Lord knows, they drilled all that stuff into us in school from the time we were little. But, looking back, I suppose, like so many of our peers, we were in a hurry to grow up and holding a cigarette had a way of making us feel older and more mature. Besides, smoking only kills older people and we both felt confident we could always quit before we ever got hooked. Besides, addictions happen to other people—not to us. We were too smart.

"Come on inside," said Uncle Bill. "You're trying to heat the whole neighbourhood and your Mom and Dad are going to wonder why it's so cold in here when they get home. Besides, I've got something out front you might want to see."

Uncle Bill led us from the kitchen, through the house and to the front door. There on the driveway stood a pristine white sports car.

"Wow!" exclaimed Logan. "A Mercedes 500SL. Holy Cow! That's some machine. I read in Motor Trends that it's worth $130,000. You must be loaded..." Logan hesitated, a bit taken aback by his own lack of couth, but Uncle Bill didn't seem to pay any mind.

"Actually," Uncle Bill said, "it didn't cost quite that much but you're not far off. It's a lot of fun though and I guess it's a just reward. I worked pretty hard in my day and I sure enjoy it. I just drove it here to store in your Mom's garage for a week or two until I move into my condo. This isn't the kind of car you'd want to drive in the Canadian winters."

"I suppose not," said Logan. "Will you take me for a drive in the spring? By then I should have my learner's permit. Maybe ..."

"We'll see," said Uncle Bill with a chuckle. "Of course I'll take you for a drive, but whether you'll be able to sit behind the wheel...I don't know. We'll have to see what the insurance is like."

"Uncle Bill," I said, "if you're going to put this car away for the winter, what are you going to do for the next few months to get around?"

"Oh," he replied, "I've got another car, a four–wheel drive Ford Explorer. It's a fabulous winter car and of course it holds a lot more than just two people. Anyway," he continued, "let's go inside. I'm freezing here. In Calgary, we'd get some pretty cold days but it was a lot less humid. I'm going to have to get used to the dampness all over again now that I'm living in the east."

We went inside and I offered Uncle Bill and Logan some hot chocolate. We closed the patio door and cranked up the heat a bit in the hope we could get the temperature in the house back up to normal before Mom and Dad came home. When we had settled down with our steaming mugs, Uncle Bill took a sip, smacked his lips and nodded a thank you in my direction.

"So," he said, "I suppose this is a bit trite, but what's new in school? I'm not all that used to dealing with young people any more, now that  your cousins are off at university so I might as well start with the usual."

"Mom said you're an accountant," Logan replied, changing the subject. "I thought accountants were boring, wore thick glasses and bow ties."

"At your age," said Uncle Bill a bit crossly, "you shouldn't be stereotyping people. Actually, the accounting profession has changed a lot over the last 25 years and you'll be amazed at the window of opportunity one has with a professional accounting designation."

"What do you mean, Uncle Bill?" I asked.

"Well," he replied, "accountants do a lot more today than slave over ledgers like Bob Cratchit did in Dickens' *'Christmas Carol'*. Nowadays, a lot of accountants are experts in computers. Others assist people to set up businesses, for example, by helping them get financing from banks and other lenders. The way they do this is by working with their clients to draft business plans that lenders can read and evaluate. Other accountants are experts in income taxes and help people save money...legitimately, I might add...so they can take home more to their families. Still others, like myself, have devoted at least part of their careers to something called financial planning."

"What's that?" asked Logan.

"Financial planning," replied Uncle Bill, "is the process whereby a family can budget for its income and expenses and set up a savings and investment program. In today's uncertain economic times, it's really up to all Canadians to look after themselves. You can't always count on government to look after you when you get older."

"We've just started a new course at school called Health and Lifestyles," I interrupted excitedly. "Our teacher, Mrs. Prewit, told us there are two main purposes of the course: first, to help us choose careers after we finish high school, and second, to teach us the basics of looking after ourselves."

"What do you mean by that?" asked Uncle Bill.

"They want us to learn how to budget for our living expenses," interjected Logan, taking over from where I had left off. "For example, last week we had an assignment where we had to find out what it would cost for a two bedroom apartment in the Ottawa area including utilities such as telephone, electricity, and heating."

"Yes," I interrupted, trying to get back onto centre stage. "We've also had some classes on nutrition and we had to compile shopping lists for a week's worth of food for a family of four. Then we had to take our shopping lists to a store and price out the cost. It's pretty scary. No wonder Mom and Dad work so hard. The average grocery bill came out to over $150 for just one week."

"And I'm sure that didn't include any allowance for

cigarettes," said Uncle Bill with a wry chuckle. "I'm glad to see the schools are starting to do more than just teach the old academic basics that I studied when I was a student ..."

"Yeah," interrupted Logan. "That's because you probably got your education in a one-room school house."

"Very funny," said Uncle Bill. "I'm not that old that I couldn't tan your hide if I was of a mind to do so. Maybe in a few years after they perfect your Health and Lifestyles course, they'll start giving classes in Respecting Your Elders."

"I was only kidding, Uncle Bill," said Logan contritely. "By the way, we just got a school project returned to us this afternoon and I got nine out of 10. I even beat Andrea for a change."

I refrained—just barely—from replying with a rude gesture. "Wait 'til the end of the term, Einstein," I said. "We'll see whose grades are better."

"Stop bickering, you two," said Uncle Bill. "So, what was your project all about?"

"I'll get it," said Logan as he jumped up from the table, almost knocking his chair over in the process.

"The purpose of the assignment," I told Uncle Bill as Logan ran out of the room, "was for us to project where we would be in ten years. In other words, where did we see ourselves? Married, single, with families, what kind of careers, and so on."

"Very interesting," said Uncle Bill as Logan returned shoving his report under our uncle's face.

Uncle Bill took a moment to flip through Logan's report. He suddenly started to chuckle.

"What's so funny?" asked Logan indignantly.

Uncle Bill shook his head and smiled. "No offence, young man. But I'm afraid your approach here is really overly simplistic."

"What do you mean?" asked Logan. "I got nine out of 10."

"Well," said Uncle Bill, "it says here that in 10 years' time, at your age 25 or 26, you expect to be married, own a home, have two children and drive a Porsche, all on an income of $70,000 a year."

"What's wrong with that?" Logan bristled. "You don't think I can make $70,000 a year by the time I'm 26?" He started to pull his report away.

"Hold on, bro," I interrupted. "Let Uncle Bill explain. You're so immature!" Logan let go of the report and reached out to punch my arm. I backed away and his hand rapped solidly against the kitchen table.

"Hold on, you two," said Uncle Bill. "If you want to have a serious conversation, I'm certainly game. But let's have a little order. Logan," he continued, putting his hand on my brother's shoulder, "I'm not suggesting you're incapable of earning $70,000 a year in 10 years. But even ignoring inflation, let's be realistic here. There are a few things you haven't considered and it's not your fault. It's probably because your teacher never told you about income taxes."

"What about income taxes?" I asked.

"Well," said Uncle Bill, "I won't bore you with all the details. For today, I'll just give you some of the basics. Please bring me some paper and something to write with."

I got up and got my uncle a pad of paper and a pencil.

"Okay," he said. "Forgive me if I lecture a bit, although I'll try to keep it simple and brief. If there's anything you don't understand, don't be afraid to ask questions. Got it?"

Logan and I both nodded.

"Right," said Uncle Bill. "As you know, the government is responsible for providing us with certain goods and services we want or need. For example, we have our health care system which, as you know just from what you've read and what you've seen on TV, is a lot better than the one they've got in the United States. Also, we provide help to the elderly, we have unemployment insurance for people who lose their jobs and welfare for those people who are incapable of working. We have our highways and roads, we have our military ..."

"We get the picture, Uncle Bill," interrupted Logan impatiently. "What's your point?"

"My point, Logan, is that doing all these things costs money and the government gets that money from people like myself and your Mom and Dad through taxes. We have two kinds of taxes. The first is consumption taxes like the GST—the Goods and Services Tax."

"Oh yeah," I said, "we know all about that. The government tacks on seven per cent to just about everything we buy and that's on top of provincial sales tax too."

"That's right," continued Uncle Bill. "The Goods and Services Tax is called a consumption tax and it applies to everybody, rich or poor, as long as each person making a purchase is buying the same item."

"You lost me there, Uncle Bill," said Logan.

"Okay," Uncle Bill replied. "I'll make it simple. If you're earning $20,000 a year and you buy a book for $10, you'll have to pay 70 cents in GST. If your sister is earning $100,000 a year and buys the same $10 book, she has to pay the same 70 cents that you do. Since her income, in my example, is five times higher than yours, you obviously suffer a lot more than she does from having to pay the GST. This is why economists and accountants, like myself, would refer to the GST as a *regressive tax*. It hits people in their pocket books to the same extent without considering whether they are rich or poor."

"But suppose I buy a Porsche," asked Logan, "and Andrea buys a Dodge Colt. Won't I pay more GST?"

"Good point, my boy," said Uncle Bill. "It's true, if you buy a more expensive article such as the sports car in your example, you'll pay more GST. But when I gave my book example, I was trying to choose a purchase that isn't really all that discretionary. Maybe a book wasn't the best example because you could say if you can't afford it, you don't necessarily *need* to buy books. But what about running shoes and socks for a growing boy or girl? Whether the parents are rich or poor, their kids still basically need the same things."

"We see your point, Uncle Bill. The GST is, as you put it, ..."

"Regressive," finished Uncle Bill.

"Now," he continued, "the GST is not the only kind of tax we have. We also have taxes on *income* and they work pretty well as follows." He picked up the pencil, bent over the pad of paper and made a little schedule.

APPROXIMATE INCOME TAX BRACKETS
FEDERAL & PROVINCIAL TAX

INCOME	TAX BRACKET
$0 - $30,000	25%
$30,000 - $60,000	40% - 45%
$60,000 - ??	45% - 55%

"Here's how this works," he explained. "When you earn income from employment or business or from your investments, the government takes approximately 25 per cent of the first $30,000. These are the combined federal and provincial taxes on this level of income. There are some special concessions if you have dependents or make donations, but, for today, I just want to get the basics across to you and I think you'll soon understand my picture."

"I see," I replied. "So if you earn $30,000, the government would take away about $7,500. Wow...That's...$625 a month!"

"What a rip-off!" exclaimed Logan.

"Wait," said Uncle Bill, "it gets worse; although, remember the government does provide us with all those services I told you about earlier. When your income reaches $30,000 and goes above that level, there's a second tax bracket that comes into play on earnings between $30,000 and $60,000. At this point, depending where you live, you can count on giving the government between 40 and 45 per cent of this *incremental* or *additional income*."

"You mean, on the next $30,000, they're going to take away more than $12,000?" I asked incredulously.

"Your math skills are pretty good," said Uncle Bill with a chuckle. "And it gets even worse. On all income over $60,000, you can count on giving the government anywhere from 45 to 55 per cent."

"So how the heck can anybody become rich?" asked Logan as his shoulders sagged.

"If you want to become rich," replied Uncle Bill, "I can show you how, but we won't get it all done this afternoon. Unfortunately, I have to start with the bad news, which is how the income tax structure in Canada is geared towards making it

18

somewhat difficult to become rich. We might as well get all the bad stuff out of the way at the start and from there on in, things can only look up."

"You mean there *is* good news?" I asked hopefully.

"Yes, there definitely is," said Uncle Bill, "although becoming wealthy takes a lot of discipline. But let's not put the cart before the horse."

"So what's your point?" asked Logan, a bit impatiently.

"I'll get to my point in a minute," said Uncle Bill, "but there is just one other technical...or sort of technical...thing I'd like to tell you. Remember I explained how economists and others refer to the GST as being *regressive,* because everybody pays the same amount on identical purchases whether they are rich or poor?"

Logan and I nodded our heads as we remembered Uncle Bill's earlier explanation.

"Well," he continued, "income taxes are defined as *progressive.* This means the more you earn, the greater a percentage of your income you pay. If you're only earning $30,000 a year or less, the government takes a much smaller percentage. On the incremental income, they take more and more because the whole system is based on ability to pay."

"I get it," said Logan. "If you earn more, you pay more."

"That's right," said Uncle Bill. "Now let's get back to your report." He tapped Logan's report with the pencil.

"Okay, you see yourself with a family, a house and a Porsche at age 26, all on an income of $70,000 a year. First of all, what does $70,000 a year mean *after-tax?*"

"Gee," said Logan, "if I'm earning $70,000, which is more than $60,000, that means the government is going to take half of it away, because I'll be in a 45 to 55 per cent tax bracket."

"It's not quite as bad as that," said Uncle Bill. "Remember, it's *not* your *whole* $70,000 that would be taxed at that high rate. It's only the income over $60,000. That's what I meant by incremental."

Logan looked puzzled and, to be honest, I wasn't all that clear myself; even though I confess my math skills were better than my brother's.

"Here," said Uncle Bill as he wrote furiously on a piece of paper. "Let's calculate Logan's income taxes on an income of $70,000."

LOGAN'S INCOME TAXES ON AN INCOME OF $70,000

On the first	$30,000 @ 25%	$ 7,500
On the next	30,000 @ 42½%	12,750
On the next	10,000 @ 50%	5,000
Totals	$70,000 (25,250/70,000 = 36%)	$25,250

"On the first $30,000, your taxes would be about 25 per cent. That's $7,500. On the next $30,000, why don't we assume an effective tax rate of 42.5 per cent—midway between 40 and 45 per cent? That's $12,750. And on the final $10,000, we'll assume a 50 per cent tax rate, which is $5,000. This means $25,250 in total taxes."

"Over $2,000 a month," I said. "That's a lot of money."

"That's right. If you take the taxes of $25,250 as a percentage of Logan's $70,000 earnings, that works out to over 36 per cent. If you then take into account GST, provincial sales taxes and taxes on a house, if Logan should choose to buy one, you can see that in total ..."

"One way or another, the government's going to take away half of what I earn," wailed Logan.

YOU'RE TOO LATE—
THE TAX MAN GOT
TO ME FIRST

20

"That's true," said Uncle Bill. "And that's the sad reality. Most Canadians work half the year to pay taxes of one sort or another. There's an organization based in Vancouver called the Fraser Institute. One of the things those guys do is, each year, they calculate what they call Tax-Freedom Day—the actual date when the average person in each province finishes paying taxes and can then consider all his or her other income for the year to belong to themselves. Depending on where you live, Tax-Freedom Day varies from some time in late June to early July."

"So what the heck's the point of working hard?" asked Logan despondently.

"How does anyone ever get anywhere?" I added.

"Like I said," Uncle Bill continued, raising his hand to stop our complaining, "I'm getting the bad news over with first. There are ways for those people who are smart enough to take advantage, to rise *above the system* and become financially secure. One of the things I'd like to show you is that being successful financially doesn't necessarily mean working *hard;* it means working *smart.* It also means learning *when* to invest and *how* to invest."

"So, to become rich you need to be a scam artist or rip-off poor workers," said Logan triumphantly. "Rich guys don't have to pay taxes. Right?"

"Wait a minute," said Uncle Bill holding up his hand again, this time to stop the locomotive from picking up too much steam. "First of all, if you want me to talk to you intelligently, you'll have to accept my premise from Day One, that *it's no sin to be wealthy.* And you don't have to be a 'bad guy' to become wealthy. I'm *not* suggesting you have to knife people in the back, or defraud the government, or get involved in shady business deals. Forget all the TV Mafia gobbledygook and let's concentrate on real life. Unfortunately, there are some things you can't really learn at school, at least not today. Although the school system is evolving for the better, for the most part, your teachers aren't entrepreneurs. They're also not wealthy people and many of them are just doing the best job they can in the hope that, when they retire, their pensions will look after them."

"Pensions?" I interrupted.

"All in due course," said Uncle Bill. "I'll explain the pension system some other time. But for now, I want you to get my main point. Your teachers are on salary. And they probably pay a disproportionate amount of tax themselves because they don't have some of the advantages that are reserved for business owners, entrepreneurs and investors. Also, the education system is not structured to reward exceptional teachers. Unless things have already changed in ways I don't know about, teachers' incomes are still based on educational qualifications and length of service— not on how much they've contributed to their students' learning. No doubt this will all change in time. The fact that they're teaching you programs in health and lifestyles is a giant step in the right direction. But it's going to take time for the system to evolve.

"Now, as you probably know, I've done pretty well for myself. In fact, if I can be a bit immodest, I'll tell you that I'm certainly well able to retire and I'm still only 45 years old. In 25 years in business and as a professional, I think I've learned a thing or two and I really wouldn't mind passing some of what I've learned on to you. By the way, although, to put it candidly, I'm quite wealthy, I also want you to know I've never, ever, knifed anyone in the back in order to make money. You *can* be a good person and have high morals and proper ethics and still do very well financially."

"I understand what you're saying, Uncle Bill," said Logan. "But I'm more than a little bit upset."

"Why's that?" Uncle Bill asked.

"Well, here I got 90 per cent on this report and you're basically telling me that my whole outlook is full of sh--."

"There's nothing really wrong with your report," Uncle Bill interrupted. "It's quite acceptable to *want* to have a house, a Porsche and a family, but it's not that simple to accomplish, and not on $70,000 a year. I'm not saying, though, that it can't be done."

"Sounds confusing to me," I said. "Can Logan have his house and Porsche or not?"

"We'll see," said Uncle Bill. "There's no reason for either one of you not to have anything you want. You may not get it as quickly as you'd like, but, in the long run, if you're willing to take some advice, I think you can certainly prosper greatly. *The key point is, the earlier you start, the faster you're going to get what you want."*

"I'm not sure I know *what* I want," I said.

"I'll tell you what," replied Uncle Bill. "We'll chat for a bit and maybe you'll be able to clarify your ideas a little bit better."

"One point, though, Uncle Bill," interjected Logan, "I understand how income taxes are going to take away $25,000 a year out of my $70,000 income at age 26, assuming I can earn that much. But you really haven't explained yet *why* I can't have a Porsche."

"Okay," said Uncle Bill. "Let's work it out."

WHY LOGAN CAN'T HAVE A PORSCHE ON $70,000 A YEAR

Projected Income		$70,000
Less:	Income taxes	(25,250)
	After-tax income	44,750
Less:	Housing costs $2,000 x 12 mo.	(24,000)
	Food costs $150 x 52 wks.	(7,800)
	Clothing allowance $2,000 x 4 people	(8,000)
Disposable income for transportation, recreation, health & personal care, etc.		$ 4,950

"Let's assume you're earning an income of $70,000 at age 26. We'll then subtract your income taxes of $25,250 and that leaves $44,750. Now, you guys did some research on what an apartment costs, including utilities. How much would that be?"

"Anywhere from $650 to $1,000 a month for a decent apartment with all costs thrown in," I said. "Of course, we learned at school we could save quite a bit by having a roommate."

"That's quite true," said Uncle Bill, "but would you bear with me and assume that, at a minimum, if an apartment costs that much, a house would cost $2,000 a month to maintain, including mortgage payments, taxes, utilities and so on?"

"Okay by me," shrugged Logan.

"Fine," said Uncle Bill. "$2,000 times 12 months is $24,000. Now," he continued turning to me, "you said that groceries for a family of four would average $150 a week."

I nodded in reply.

"Times 52 weeks, that works out to $7,800. What else do we have to consider?"

"Clothes!" I said triumphantly.

"Exactly," replied Uncle Bill. "Let's assume an annual family clothing allowance of $2,000 for each person. So, for a husband, a wife and two kids, that's $8,000 a year. Now, if we subtract housing, food and clothing from an after-tax income of $44,750, that leaves just under $5,000 as extra disposable income—and that has to cover transportation, recreation, health and personal care, and any other expenses you might incur, such as life insurance."

"I can see that $70,000 a year isn't all it's cracked up to be," said Logan dejectedly. "You're right, there's no way I'd ever have a Porsche on that income."

"Well, it's a question of priorities," said Uncle Bill. "Unfortunately, the sad reality is that sometimes having certain luxuries is inconsistent with trying to raise a family. If you were a single person, living in an apartment, earning $70,000 a year, you probably *could* afford a Porsche. Instead of making house payments, you'd be making car payments, but that's what your priority would be."

"But I want it *all*," wailed Logan.

"He just wants to play house with Sandy Lavigne!" I exclaimed, enjoying seeing my brother squirm.

"Oh yeah?" said Logan. "Who's ever going to want to play house with you, big sister?"

"Hold on, you guys," said Uncle Bill raising his hands in exasperation. "Are we mature adults here, or what?"

"What!" Logan and I exclaimed in unison.

"We're yo-ads, my dear uncle," I said with a bow.

"Yo-ads?" repeated Uncle Bill suspiciously.

"Yes, young adults," said Logan proudly.

"Everything today is abbreviated. Yo-ads. That's a neat term," Uncle Bill said with a chuckle. "I'll have to remember that."

Just then we heard noises at the front door. Mom and Dad had just arrived.

"Listen, you two," said Uncle Bill, "I've got some time tomorrow afternoon. Perhaps you'd like to continue this conversation then. I think we might do better in private."

"I think you're right," said Logan. "Dad's always been jealous of Mom's brother."

"Logan!" I said. "You're not supposed to ..."

"That's okay, kids, oh excuse me, yo-ads," said Uncle Bill. "I understand. Why don't we meet here tomorrow around 4:00 and I'll give you two the *good* news? I think I did enough today to shatter some of your illusions and I'd really like the opportunity to show you that your futures can be a lot brighter than the picture I painted today."

"Fine with me, Uncle Bill," said Logan, as I nodded my head in agreement as well.

Just then, Mom and Dad came into the kitchen and we adjourned our meeting.

CHAPTER THREE

LOGAN'S STORY: THE NEXT DAY...

THE NEXT AFTERNOON at 4:00 we got home from school, and there in the living room, true to his word, stood Uncle Bill with a book in his hand. We ushered him into the kitchen, where it was my turn to make hot chocolate. He sat down at the table, flipping the book he was holding on its back with a flourish so that Andrea and I couldn't read the cover.

"What's that, Uncle Bill?" asked Andrea, pointing at the book.

"Patience," replied Uncle Bill. "All in due time."

I distributed three mugs of hot chocolate and sat down next to my uncle. Suddenly, his nose crinkled and he sniffed a couple of times.

"Logan," he said to me, "I didn't say anything yesterday, but I gather you've been smoking again. Now, I know it's cool to smoke, and, at your age, you feel invincible, so no matter what they tell you in school or what you read, you can't visualize the dangers. Also, if you smoke a couple of cigarettes a day, I know it really does taste good and makes you feel good. But then, eventually, you get hooked and before you know it you're up to a pack a day and you start coughing."

"How do you know all this?" asked Andrea.

"Well, I have to confess I used to smoke, although I quit 'cold turkey' back in 1977. Friday the 13th of May, to be exact. I'd been coughing for quite a long time, especially in the mornings, and on that day, I went down to Burlington, Vermont, with a client of mine, who was looking to buy a business. I sat in his car all day long and smoked like a chimney because I had nothing

27

else to do. By the time I got home, my throat felt like sandpaper and I had one hell of a headache. I just tossed the rest of my pack away and never picked one up since.

"But," he continued, "the health stuff is not really what I want to get at. Yesterday, you guys told me you were at least a little bit curious about how someone becomes wealthy. Today I'm going to show you how it really isn't all that hard, as long as you make some important lifestyle decisions—the earlier the better. I told you yesterday that the idea of building wealth and having a family might create a conflict. *But it doesn't have to be that way.* Believe it or not, *especially if you start at your age, all you have to do to become wealthy is avoid some bad habits.*"

"What do you mean, Uncle Bill?" I asked.

"If you make a conscious decision that you're not going to smoke and that you'll try and stay away as much as possible from buying junk food, and when you get a little older, you don't develop the habit of stopping off after work for a drink or two, that's really all you're going to have to do to become wealthy. If you just invest the money you save...."

"You're joking!" exclaimed Andrea. "Even if Logan smoked a pack a day, or I spent every night at a club with my girlfriends, nursing a couple of drinks and listening to music, what difference could that possibly make?"

"All the difference in the world," replied Uncle Bill with a chuckle. "Now I'm not suggesting that to become wealthy, you have to lead a boring life. I don't smoke, and generally limit myself to one or two glasses of wine with dinner about three times a week, but I certainly wouldn't describe my life as dull. At my age," he continued, patting himself on the stomach, "I have to stay away from junk food or I'd be floating up to your ceiling like a balloon. Making it a policy to stay in good shape isn't a bad thing to do as well. In fact, I've joined the Elgin Health Club, and expect to go there at least every other day for a work-out."

"Okay," I interrupted a bit impatiently. "It's obviously better for our health if we don't smoke or drink a lot, and if we stay away from junk food. But you can't tell us that simply investing the money we'd save is going to make us wealthy."

"I can so," said Uncle Bill. "And better than that, I can prove it to you—with the help of this little book here." He reached out and flipped the book over right-side up.

"*'Henry B. Zimmer's Money Manager For Canadians. The Practical Guide to Making Your Money Grow'*," read Andrea.

"Uggh," I interrupted. "Sounds pretty boring to me."

"I gather," said Uncle Bill, "that math isn't one of your strong suits. But look at the top right-hand corner where it says *'you don't have to be a mathematical genius!'*. The guy who wrote this, Henry Zimmer, is a Calgary-based accountant like myself, who for many years lectured in income tax at the University of Calgary. When he and I took mathematics of finance courses as part of our accounting training, way back in the dark ages, the people who taught those courses were only interested in drumming formulas into our heads. They never explained the *practical applications* of what you could do with some of these formulas." Uncle Bill's eyes glazed over as he began to reminisce. "I remember when I took a math exam, I have to confess I would write some of these formulas down on my arm in pen the morning of the exam and then wear long sleeves to the classroom. I used to pray for cold rainy days in May and June so nobody would question my choice of attire. I have to tell you though, I never peeked at what I'd written. Somehow or other, just writing those formulas down and knowing I had the opportunity to cheat was good enough. Somehow they stuck in my head. I guess there must be a link between my arms and my brain."

"Sure thing, Uncle Bill," I said laughing. "But what's this thing all about?" I continued, pointing at the book.

"Oh, yes," replied Uncle Bill as his eyes began to focus once more on the here and now. "What this Zimmer guy did was to take all these mathematics formulas and create a bunch of simple, easy-to-use tables. Then he wrote this book in which he actually explains how to use the tables to make business and investment decisions. For example, take a look at Table 1." Uncle Bill opened the book to the middle. "Table 1," he continued, "is called 'The Compound Amount of $1'. What this table allows you to do is answer the following question: if I invest $1 today, at different rates of return, what will I have at the end of so many years? For example, let's assume you can earn 12 per cent on your money."

"How so, Uncle Bill?" Andrea interrupted. "I happen to know the banks are only paying three or four per cent."

"That's true for today," said Uncle Bill, "but all in due time. I'll show you how you can do a lot better than three or four per cent. Bear with me for the moment, so I can illustrate what I'm trying to show you." Andrea nodded and we both peered at Uncle Bill's book.

"Okay, here we are on page 131. Let's assume you invest $1 and you can earn 12 per cent compounded annually."

"I have to confess, Uncle Bill," I interrupted, "I really don't know what you mean by 'compounded'."

"What a dummy. Where were you during English class?" interrupted Andrea disgustedly.

"Now, hang on a second," Uncle Bill said sternly, "the fact that you don't know something doesn't make you a dummy. As long as you're willing to learn, that makes you pretty smart in my books. There's a big difference between ignorance and stupidity."

"I'm sorry, Logan," Andrea replied contritely.

"Actually," said Uncle Bill switching into lecture mode, "the concept of compounding is not that difficult. It's simply where you earn income, not only on your original deposit, but also on the accumulated income from previous years. Here, take another look at this table. If you invest $1 at 12 per cent, at the end of one year what would you have?"

"$1.12," I replied.

"That's right," said Uncle Bill nodding his head. "Now, what would you have after two years on that same dollar?"

"$1.24," I answered triumphantly.

"That's wrong," said Uncle Bill with a smile. "If you were earning simple interest at 12 per cent on your dollar, you would have $1.24. But if you're earning compound income, remember, in the second year, you'd earn not only 12 per cent on your original dollar, but you'd also earn that same 12 per cent on the

12 cents you earned in the first year. If you look at the second number in this column, you can actually see you'd have a little more than $1.25 in place of your $1. Similarly, at the end of three years, you would have $1.40 instead of only $1.36."

THE COMPOUND AMOUNT OF $1

12% INTEREST COMPOUNDED ANNUALLY	
End of Year	
1	1.120
2	1.254
3	1.405
4	1.574
5	1.762
10	3.106
20	9.646
30	29.960
40	93.051
50	289.002

"I think I get it," I said. "Earning compound income, in this case interest, simply means earning income *on* your income."

"Exactly," Uncle Bill said, patting me on the shoulder. "Over the first few years, earning compound income isn't all that exciting," he continued. "After all, does it really make a difference whether, after three years, you have $1.36 or $1.40? But look what happens to $1 left alone to compound income at 12 per cent after ten years." He pointed part way down the page.

"Wow," said Andrea.

"After 10 years, $1 more than triples; and look what happens after 30 years," Uncle Bill said nodding his head and turning the book in my direction.

"After 30 years, $1 invested at 12 per cent comes to almost $30," I said. "But what's the point, $30 doesn't make you rich." I still didn't see the big picture.

"Of course not," said Uncle Bill. "But let me give you a practical application." He reached into the pocket of his jacket and pulled out a little calculator. "This book and a small hand-held calculator are basically all that virtually anybody needs to make business or investment decisions," he said with a smile.

"Let's just assume you had $5,000 in 10 years' time at your age 25," he said to me.

"How would I ..."

Uncle Bill raised his hand like a traffic cop, interrupting me in mid-sentence. "How you get the $5,000 is something we'll talk about a bit later on. For now, let's just assume you have $5,000 at age 25. Can you bear with me on that?"

"Sure, Uncle Bill," I said shrugging my shoulders.

"Well, then," he continued. "Let's assume you had $5,000 at age 25 and *never saved another penny*. You then took that $5,000 and invested it for 40 years and left it alone. And let's assume you could earn 12 per cent on your money. What would you have when you retired at age 65?"

"Beats me," I said, puzzled.

"It's easy," said Andrea taking the calculator from Uncle Bill. "If $1 amounts to $93.051 after 40 years, then $5,000 amounts to 5000 times 93.051." She quickly punched the figures into the calculator. "I don't believe it!" she said.

"How much is it?" I grabbed the calculator out of her hand. "You must have misplaced a decimal somewhere," I said disbelievingly.

Uncle Bill looked at the number. "No," he said. "She did it quite correctly. $465,255."

"That's almost half a million dollars," I said incredulously.

"That's right," replied Uncle Bill. "A single, one-time investment at age 25 of $5,000 earning 12 per cent a year would give you almost a half-million dollars at age 65. So, what would happen if you were age 25, Logan, and you had $5,000 and you married someone who was also age 25 who also had $5,000, and the two of you had enough discipline not to touch your investment capital until you retired?"

"My goodness," I answered, "we'd have a million bucks. Then ... but ... why isn't everybody rich?"

"People aren't rich because they don't set their goals properly. They don't have a plan," replied Uncle Bill. "A lot of people buy lottery tickets in the hope that *luck* will make them rich. Sure luck is important. Being in the right place at the right time

certainly helps, but *you have to have a plan.* $5,000 is no great fortune to start with. And you certainly don't have to be a mean-spirited, ruthless business-tycoon to accumulate that kind of money at a relatively early age. But it does take a plan."

"By the way, Uncle Bill," Andrea interrupted, "$5,000 may not be a lot to you, but it is to us. Where would we ever get that kind of money?"

"Again, all in due time," replied Uncle Bill. "Just for fun though, Logan, why don't you calculate what you would have at age 65 if you happened to have $5,000 *right now* and you invested it at 12 per cent without touching it for 50 years."

"Let's see," I said as I looked down the table. "$1 left alone to compound at 12 per cent for 50 years amounts to $289 even. So, $5,000 is 5000 times 289. $1,445,000."

"Are you sure you haven't got an extra $5,000 to spare, Uncle Bill?" Andrea said nudging him in the ribs.

"I do," said Uncle Bill, "but I'm not going to give it to you. I think, in the long run, you'll get a lot more satisfaction out of making it on your own."

"Yeah, right," I said sarcastically.

"But it's not impossible," said Andrea. "I'm amazed that everybody isn't rich."

"You two have the opportunity to be exceptions, although, quite frankly, the way things are going, I suspect that more and more young people will, in fact, be encouraged to look after their own financial futures over the next few years. This health and lifestyles program you've got at school is certainly a big step in the right direction. Once the school boards take *the next step*, there are going to be a lot more motivated young people."

"What next step?" Andrea asked, a puzzled expression on her face.

"Oh, I alluded to that earlier. The schools still teach mathematics from a theoretical point of view, with an emphasis on formulas instead of practical applications. Once they clue in on *the real-life approach* I'm showing you here, it'll be a whole new ball game. By the way, some institutions offer investment choices that will compound your income monthly, or even daily.

The results at the end are even better. It just takes shopping around."

"But if everybody knew about this," I said pouting, "Andrea and I won't be special when *we're* wealthy."

"To me, you'll always be special," replied Uncle Bill. "Besides," he said, "let's be practical. You know the old cliche, 'you can lead a horse to water but you can't make it drink'. Unfortunately, there are always going to be people who won't be willing to focus sufficiently to plan for their futures. Hopefully, though, their numbers will diminish. But now, I want to take just a few more minutes to introduce you to another concept that's even more important than the compound growth of a single one-time investment."

"What's that, Uncle Bill?" asked Andrea.

"*The real key to achieving wealth is not to simply have, say, $5,000 as a single lump-sum investment at a young age. The important thing is to have a regular savings and investment program.* In other words, in the long run, you'll be much further ahead if you save, say, $200 a month for many, many years rather than just simply accumulating a relatively small single lump-sum and letting it ride. When you start earning money, whether it's from a job or your own business, you have to learn to *pay yourself first!*"

"What do you mean 'pay yourself first'?" I asked.

I'D LIKE TO OPEN A NEW ACCOUNT — PREFERABLY ONE WITH SOME MONEY IN IT

Wicks

"You must get into the habit," continued Uncle Bill, "of setting aside a sum of money every single month, like clockwork, on a regular basis. For example, say you're all grown up and you're earning $3,000 a month and you decide you're going to save 10 per cent of your earnings. ***Every month you have to put aside $300, and you have to treat your savings as if they were an expense, just like your rent or your mortgage payment.*** I know it's a little tough to follow at first, but we'll go through all this again and I don't think it'll take too long before it becomes clear to you. What I want to focus on now is the basic concept of putting aside a certain amount of money *every single month on a regular basis* as opposed to just making a one-time investment."

"Okay, Uncle Bill," I said. "So where do we go from here?"

"Back to this book," replied Uncle Bill, picking up *'The Money Manager'*. "Here is the second table at the back of the book called 'The Future Value of $1 Invested at the End of Each Period'. Let's again look at what happens if you can earn 12 per cent on your money."

THE FUTURE VALUE OF $1 INVESTED
AT THE END OF EACH PERIOD

12% INTEREST COMPOUNDED AND DEPOSITS MADE MONTHLY	
End of Year	
1	12.683
2	26.973
3	43.077
4	61.223
5	81.670
10	230.039
20	989.255
30	3,494.964
40	11,764.773
50	39,058.340

"Now, in this case, we'll assume you invest $1 every single month and your income also compounds monthly. Without looking, if you put aside $1 a month, Logan, how much do you think you'll have after one year?"

"Oh, that must be a trick question. $12, of course."

"What about the interest, genius?" interjected Andrea.

"Right," I said, fixing my sister with a dirty look. "You'd get interest on each deposit. But I don't know quite how to work that out, short of making the calculations long-hand: $1 earning income for 12 months, the second dollar earning income for 11 months, and so on."

"As you might expect," interrupted Uncle Bill, "there's a formula that'll work this out for you. But here's the beauty of 'The Money Manager'. If you look at this table, you can see at the end of one year, you'd have $12.68. The 68 cents would represent your interest. Then, at the end of two years, if you continue to put aside $1 a month, instead of having only $24, you'd have almost $27."

"I see how it works."

"Now, the mind-boggling thing ... and this takes some getting used to...is look what $1 a month would give you after 10 years."

"Wow," said Andrea, "$230."

"Logan," asked Uncle Bill, "what about after 40 years?"

"$1 a month after 40 years comes to $11,764. Get real! That's not possible! You mean anybody who puts aside $1 a month for 40 years could have enough money to buy a car at the end?"

"That's right," Uncle Bill said nodding.

"Of course, I'd be too old to enjoy it if I had to wait 'til then," I said.

"One step at a time, Logan," replied Uncle Bill. "I'm not suggesting anywhere that you have to save every penny you earn. I don't suppose it's a lot of fun to wait until you're 55 to start enjoying things. Obviously, a balanced investment program would include some rewards along the way. Did you guys ever read 'The Popcorn Report'?"

"As a matter of fact," said Andrea, "our social studies teacher recommended it to us when we discussed emerging trends in the latter part of the 20th Century. In fact, I have a copy upstairs."

"It's an interesting book," Uncle Bill said. "Remember, where she talks about small indulgences?"

"Sure," said Andrea excitedly. "Even Mom fits into the kind

of mind-set that Ms. Popcorn talks about. I've overheard her many times telling her friends that, when she feels depressed, she goes out and buys some new lingerie."

"Exactly," said Uncle Bill with a chuckle. "That's a good example of a small indulgence. So, for now, one of the key things to keep in mind, if you're interested in continuing these talks ..."

"We sure are, Uncle Bill," I said.

"No doubt," interjected Andrea.

"Well, okay," said Uncle Bill, "like I say, if you want to continue these talks we should always keep in mind that *a savings program won't give you a whole lot of satisfaction unless you also have a well-thought-out spending program. You've got to enjoy yourself along the way, or the whole exercise of becoming wealthy isn't worthwhile.* Fortunately, you two guys are young enough to have it all...as long as you've got some discipline."

"Uncle Bill," I asked, "you talked about saving and spending. Isn't there something you're missing?"

"What's that?"

"Earning. We have to *earn money* before we can save and before we can spend. What do you have to say about that?"

"All in due course, Logan. Rome wasn't built in a day, as they say. We'll look at earnings next. But before we do, let's just go back to that little calculation of the future value of $1. Remember, earlier on, I lectured you on smoking, drinking, and junk food? Let's assume you were a heavy smoker and you smoked a pack a day. I don't know exactly what a package of cigarettes costs but let's assume it's about $5, more or less. Naturally, the price of tobacco keeps going up, mainly because of government taxes. Do you think it's reasonable to assume that over the next 10, 20 or even 30 years, the price of a package of cigarettes will average, say, $6.50?"

"Sounds reasonable to me," I said.

"Agreed," added Andrea.

"Okay. Let's take a person who smokes a pack a day at an average cost of $6.50. That's $200 a month that goes up in smoke. *By the way, one could easily spend the same $200 going out for a drink or two after work five days a week; or, for that matter, buying junk food every day."*

"I suppose you're right. So, what's your point?" asked Andrea.

"Well, what do you think you'd have if, instead of wasting that money on tobacco, alcohol, or junk food, you took $200 a month and socked it away at 12 per cent? First, let's look at 10 years. Let's assume you could earn $200 a month, starting now, which you didn't waste, and you put it away. What would you have at the end of 10 years?"

"I dunno," I said.

"Just look at the table, Logan. If $1 invested each month for 10 years amounts to $230, what would $200 a month come to?" Uncle Bill handed me his calculator.

"I guess the answer is 200 times 230." I rapidly keyed in the figures. "$46,000! You mean, if I put aside $200 a month starting now, by my age 26 I'd have $46,000? That's a fortune!"

"It's not a fortune," said Uncle Bill, "but it sure is a lot more than you'd have if you burned up a package of cigarettes a day in smoke. Now, let's look at 20 years. Andrea, you do the honours."

"Well, let's see," she said. "989 times $200. No ... $197,800?"

"That's right," said Uncle Bill. "Now, the big question. What about 30 years? What if you started saving $200 a month as of today, what would you have when you're my age?"

"False teeth and a cane?" I answered sweetly.

"Very funny, kid," Uncle Bill replied gruffly. "I'll bet I can still wrestle you to the ground."

"That's only because you out-weigh me by 60 pounds," I answered jokingly.

"Really, Logan," said Andrea. "Uncle Bill's not old, he's just one of the big kids. And he's in a lot better shape than Dad."

"That's true," Uncle Bill replied. "I suppose it's because I don't have to work as hard as your Dad, and when you don't have stress, I think, in general, you don't age as quickly. Today, I admit I probably look pretty old to you guys, but it won't be long before you're sitting here in my shoes. You'll be amazed how quickly time passes. It seems like only yesterday I was your age and I would've been really, really happy to have had someone teach *me* what I think I can teach *you*."

"You're right, Uncle Bill. Sorry for the bad jokes," I said.

"Believe me, Andrea and I appreciate what you're doing. This is really cool, man."

"Okay," said Uncle Bill. "Where were we? Oh yes. What if you put aside $200 a month for 30 years starting now? What would you have at age 45?" Andrea grabbed the calculator out of my hand.

"$200 times 3,495. $699,000! Wow! *That's* a fortune. We'd be rich."

"You'd certainly be in the top 10 per cent of all Canadians."

"Yeah," I said, "but what about all this inflation stuff I keep hearing about?"

"We'll talk about inflation another day. For now, let me just share something with you."

"Go ahead," I said, "I'm all ears."

"That he is," said Andrea. I reached out and punched her none too gently on the shoulder. Uncle Bill glared at me and the horseplay stopped.

"Let's assume," he said, "you had $1,000,000 in 30 years' time. What about inflation? Have you guys ever read any books that are set, say, at the beginning of the 20th Century?"

"Sure," I said shrugging my shoulders.

"What if you were to read a book set in that time period and a character in the book was described as being a millionaire? How would you picture that person?"

"Rich," said Andrea.

"Exactly. Now, what if today we were walking in the street and I pointed someone out and I said, 'see that person, he or she is a millionaire'. What would your reaction be?"

"Rich," I replied.

"Exactly my point!" said Uncle Bill. "In spite of over 90 years of inflation, a millionaire today is still considered wealthy, the same as a millionaire was in the year 1900. Relatively few people can claim that distinction and all I can say is: *inflation-be-damned. I'd rather have $1,000,000 than not have $1,000,000.* One last point, though."

"What's that?" asked Andrea.

"Let's assume you started saving $200 a month today at age

15, without increasing or decreasing that amount for 50 years until your age 65—not even taking into account that, as you get older, you start to earn more and you could conceivably save more than $200 on a monthly basis. So, what do you think $200 a month for 50 years would come to?"

"I can work that out," I said, as I, in turn, grabbed the calculator from my sister. "$200 times 39,058. I don't believe it. $7,811,600."

Andrea's mouth dropped open.

"That's right," said Uncle Bill. "Now you understand the power of compound income. I know you can't get that kind of return today by simply putting your money in the bank. There's also income taxes to contend with. But in the not too distant future, I'll explain to you how a return such as this *is* viable."

"But, Uncle Bill," I interjected, "you still haven't explained how we're going to *earn money*. We can't save what we don't have."

"Ah," said Uncle Bill, "I think we've done enough for one day and, quite frankly, I've got to run along. I have a dinner date and I have to get ready for it." He blushed slightly.

"Who with, Uncle Studly?" I asked.

"Oh, never mind," he said. "In due course, if something develops, you'll meet her. But anyway, I've got to run. Listen, I've got an idea. I've got three tickets to tomorrow night's hockey game. The Senators are playing the Flames. How would you guys like to go see the game?"

"We'd love it!" Andrea and I answered in unison.

"I warn you, though," said Uncle Bill. "I'm still a big Flames fan. So you'd better get ready for some razzing."

"Don't worry, Uncle Bill," I said, "we'll protect you against the die-hard Ottawa fans."

"I'm not really worried," said Uncle Bill, "but you can bet I'll be wearing my red and yellow sweater."

"We'll just have to pretend we don't know you," I replied.

"Right," said Uncle Bill. "Kidding aside, why don't we meet here tomorrow after school? We can talk a bit about earning money so you can start to save and invest it, and then we'll go for a bite to eat before the game. We should have an hour or so to talk and then we'll trot off. Oh, do you think I should clear all this with your Mom?"

"Don't worry, Uncle Bill," said Andrea. "Mom will welcome the opportunity not to cook. If I know her, she'll convince Dad to take her out to dinner and it'll probably do them some good to have a few hours without us around."

"Okay, then. It's a deal. I'll see you tomorrow," said Uncle Bill as he got up from the table, clutching his calculator and copy of 'The Money Manager'.

AND WHILE IT'S TRUE THAT OUR LORD NEVER HAD TO CONCERN HIMSELF WITH RATES OF RETURN ON INTEREST.

CHAPTER FOUR

ANDREA'S STORY: HOCKEY NIGHT IN CANADA

IN THOSE DAYS, the Ottawa Senators certainly weren't a force to be reckoned with. In fact, to put it crudely, next to the Anaheim Mighty Ducks, they were the doormat of the league. They were still a good dozen years away from making a decent showing, and a full 15 years away from their first of two consecutive Stanley Cup victories. On that momentous evening in February, 1995, when Uncle Bill took Logan and myself to our first game together, their fabulous goalie, Claude Dupont, was just barely out of diapers. For Logan and me, it was a momentous evening because, looking back, we got our first taste of what was to become our work ethic. It took us a little time, though, to appreciate Uncle Bill's concept of working smart not hard—but I guess I'm getting a bit ahead of myself in this story.

That afternoon, Uncle Bill came into the kitchen at the stroke of 4:00 wearing his red and yellow 'Flaming C' jersey. Logan groaned.

"You weren't really serious, Uncle Bill, about wearing that jersey tonight?"

"You betcha," Uncle Bill exclaimed.

"They're gonna stone us."

"Don't tell me the Ottawa Senators really have fans," Uncle Bill said in a mocking tone. "In fact, if the Prime Minister is smart, the government will abolish the darn Senate anyway and then your miserable excuse for a hockey team will have to change its name."

Uncle Bill didn't realize it at that time, but he had actually uttered in jest what almost turned out to be a prophecy. In fact, the Senate wasn't really abolished until eight years later and then, in one of the first computer referendums, the citizens of the Ottawa region voted narrowly to retain the name of their hockey club. By that time, the team was starting to emerge as a powerhouse and was becoming a force to be reckoned with, although they were beaten that year in the quarter-finals by the Stockholm Timberwolves. (As you may have guessed, I'm a big hockey fan—even more so than my brother. I often wonder if it weren't for Uncle Bill, whether I could've afforded my season's tickets on the blueline—a small indulgence??)

"I'll make the hot chocolate today," Uncle Bill said. "It's starting to snow out there and I think we should try to leave in about an hour or so. Maybe we'd be better off getting some hot dogs at the game, rather than trying to go out for dinner."

"Are you trying to increase your personal wealth at our expense?" Logan asked with mock seriousness.

"At the price they charge for hot dogs—highly unlikely," replied Uncle Bill. "Besides you should never look a gift-horse in the mouth."

"You know I'm only joking," Logan said.

"Of course," Uncle Bill replied. "Anyhow, let's get down to work. In the last couple of days, we've talked about saving and investing but perhaps the most important question is: *where is your money going to come from in the first place?* Obviously, the two of you need to explore your opportunities to earn income."

"I think we should get part-time jobs, Uncle Bill," I said, and Logan nodded his head in agreement.

"For now," Uncle Bill acknowledged with a chuckle, "I think, that's a good idea, although, I suspect within a short period of time you're going to want to look at something a little bit more creative."

"Creative?" I asked.

"Yep," replied Uncle Bill. "There are better ways to make a living than working for somebody else. But just to get your feet wet, let's look at a job, at least for the short-term."

"I've got an idea," said Logan.

"Hang on to it," I replied. "It doesn't happen too often." Uncle Bill reached in to intercept Logan's jab.

"Let's hear it, Logan," he said.

"I was talking to Rajab Patel at school today. He's got a job delivering papers for the Ottawa Times-Herald. He told me his supervisor said they were looking for paper carriers in our district. I asked him how much we could make and he said about $200 a month. Basically, the job requires about an hour and a half each day, six days a week. He calculated it's about $5 an hour. Then, as a bonus, there can be some pretty nice tips at Christmas time. The only drawback is you gotta get up at about 6:00 every morning to get all the deliveries done before school starts."

"Uggh," I said. "6:00? That's barbaric."

"Perhaps so," said Uncle Bill, "but if you want to earn money at this stage of your lives—and I've already convinced you that earlier is better than later—you're going to have to give up something. *You can either work before school or after school, so it's basically a question of giving up sleep or sitcoms.*"

"You've got quite a way with words, Uncle Bill," I said. "What do you mean 'sleep or sitcoms'?"

"It's simple," he replied. "You either get up early in the morning and work at a job before school, or you do your work in the evenings and perhaps on weekends, which means you don't watch TV. I may sound like an old fogey to you and you don't have to take my advice if you don't want to. But if I were you, I'd simply cancel TV and that includes Nintendo, from my life. You'll be amazed how productive you can be if you don't spend two or three hours a night, and probably double that on weekends, watching the tube.

"I don't mean there shouldn't be exceptions. I'm the first to admit I'm glued to the TV when the Stanley Cup finals come on and I like to watch the World Series. But most of the time, I'd rather *do* something than be a couch potato.

"I'll tell you a little story: There used to be a telephone commercial that ran in conjunction with the hockey playoff games featuring a Canadian actor by the name of Larry Mann. He was a heavy-set fellow with bushy eyebrows. The gist of the commercial was that he played the boss of a company who ended up complimenting his employees for using the telephone for making long-distance calls, rather than the more expensive alternative of travelling. He used to pat his employees on the back for saving the company money.

"One time, Larry was in Calgary on a telephone company promotion tour and I happened to be introduced to him at a party. I didn't know who he was by name, so I said to him, 'You look just like the guy who does those commercials on TV.' The person who introduced me said, 'He is.' At that point, Larry's wife interjected and told me Larry was going to be on *Hill Street Blues* the following season. I looked at her and said 'What's that?' Everyone stared at me as if I had just descended from Mars. But I honestly had no idea *Hill Street Blues* was a popular television weekly drama. To tell you the truth, though, I wasn't the slightest bit embarrassed.

"I'll bet you if the average Canadian watched *half* the TV he or she does, and used the time saved to earn just minimum wage, the investment of those dollars would be enough to ensure a comfortable retirement, and I don't think I'm exaggerating."

"C'mon, Uncle Bill," Logan said. "A guy's gotta unwind, doesn't he?"

"Of course," Uncle Bill replied. "There are some really good shows on TV that I do confess I've watched from time to time, especially since I sold my business. *W5* for example, and *60 Minutes*. And there are some interesting specials. But, in the same way I recommend you don't get hooked on tobacco or alcohol, I wouldn't get hooked on sitcoms or Nintendo. Besides," he chuckled, "after a couple of weeks of getting up early in the morning to deliver papers, you guys are going to want to get to bed a lot earlier than you do now."

Logan turned to me and asked, "So, Sis, do you want to give the paper route idea a whirl?"

"I suppose so," I answered. "I guess we don't have a whole lot to lose. Let's try it. It'll be fun to earn some money for a change."

"Good," Logan replied. "I've got Rajab's supervisor's name

and phone number upstairs. I'll call him and make an appointment."

"Go for it," said Uncle Bill. "We still have a few minutes before we have to leave for the game. I look forward to the day when you guys take *me* out for the evening and I can introduce you to people as my niece and nephew: The Wealthy Paper Carriers!"

Chapter Five
March 1995
Logan's Story: Hi Ho, Hi Ho,
It's Off to Work We Go

THAT EVENING, before leaving for the hockey game, I managed to reach Al Quinn, Rajab's supervisor at the Times-Herald, on the telephone. I arranged a meeting with him for Andrea and myself for the next day after school. It was all pretty easy because Rajab told us what to expect at our interview—Andrea and I had grabbed him at lunchtime and had pumped him with all kinds of questions. Rajab again confirmed that, in exchange for a bit of sleep, we could each earn about $200 a month—at that time a vast fortune. He told us Mr. Quinn would ask us about previous work experience, of which we had none. He advised us to go to Miss Lalonde, our class guidance counsellor, for a letter of reference.

"If you don't have work experience," he told us, "a letter of reference from a teacher or principal is the next best thing."

Fortunately, Miss Lalonde was happy to oblige. Andrea and I didn't really realize this at the time, but, looking back, there's a valuable lesson to be learned: *if you're going to go for a job interview, the better prepared you are and the more you know about the job, the better your chances of getting it.*

I confess neither Andrea nor I had enough 'class' to buy Rajab a pop as a thank you for all he did to help us. We did make it up to him though a few years ago, when we saw each other for the first time at our 15th anniversary class reunion. Dr. Patel came in from Vancouver where he's the youngest medical director in the history of the prestigious Vancouver General Hospital. Andrea, Rajab and myself, together with our spouses, enjoyed a fabulous dinner at the Chateau Laurier and Andrea and I split the tab.

So, in the end, we got the jobs all right, although I won't pretend the follow-through was easy. It was damn tough getting up early in the morning and, in fact, we soon found the latest we could set our alarms for was 5:30, not 6:00. Also, delivering papers in the early morning during Canadian winters wasn't the most fun thing Andrea and I could think of doing! Believe me, we complained a lot. But after the first week or two, we started to adjust and, within a month, we were comfortably into a routine.

Uncle Bill wasn't around those first couple of weeks. He had decided to take a little holiday and was off somewhere in the Caribbean with a lady friend. I wonder if his ears were burning at some of the things Andrea and I said about him for getting us into this work scene in the first place.

Mom and Dad were sure pleased with us, although Mom fretted over a possible decline in our grades. Dad drove us nuts with his constant references to having us support him in his old age. But with all our complaining, we had to admit Uncle Bill was right. Basically, our cost of earning money was about an hour or so of TV a night. We simply went to bed that much earlier than before.

Then came that fabulous Monday morning at the end of March. I can still remember it as if it were yesterday. There was a hint of warmth in the air, even at 6:00 in the morning when Andrea and I trudged over to Mr. Quinn's house to pick up our daily allotment of papers. The snowbanks had shrunk significantly and there were even patches of dry concrete on the sidewalks. Mr. Quinn met us at the door and handed us each an envelope.

"Don't lose this, kids," he said with a smile.

It was our first paycheques! Instead of splitting up as we normally did, Andrea and I lingered until Mr. Quinn had shut the door behind him. Without a word, we ripped open our respective envelopes. I had made $211.30 and Andrea's pay was $207.40. We smiled broadly and gave each other high-fives. There wasn't much time for rejoicing though, because we had our deadline to meet. We shoved our cheques back into our pockets and trudged off on our daily routes.

We didn't have much opportunity to talk before lunch that day, but I'll bet each of us must've pulled those hard earned cheques from our pockets a dozen times or more during the course of that morning.

"Logan, what should we do with the money?" Andrea asked me.

"Beats the heck out of me," I answered. "I guess we put it in the bank."

"Maybe we should talk to Uncle Bill. Mom said he came home from his holiday the day before yesterday and he and his girlfriend would be going out for dinner with Mom and Dad on Friday. I'll call him. I've got his phone number in my bag."

Andrea left me at the lunch table and returned a couple of minutes later.

"We're in luck," she said. "I caught Uncle Bill at home and he's offered to take us out for dinner tonight to that new Italian place, Chianti, to celebrate our first paycheques. He said he'll pick us up at 6:00 so we'll still be home in time to do some homework before bed. I'll call Mom at work and tell her we won't be home for dinner."

"All right!" I exclaimed enthusiastically. "Monday night. All you can eat spaghetti!"

Just then a shadow fell across our table. Our little party was being interrupted. It was Dave 'The Hulk' Parker from Grade 12.

"You two guys wanna buy some smokes?" he asked.

"No, thank you," Andrea said.

"I can give ya a real good deal," he said. "I borrowed a carton from my Dad's grocery store."

"No thanks, Dave, we'll pass," I said firmly. "But thanks for thinking of us." He shrugged his shoulders and walked away.

"Quite the little diplomat you are," my sister said to me with a smile.

"I suppose it doesn't hurt to be polite," I said. "Besides, if I'd just told him to beat it, he could easily have beaten the living daylights out of me. I thought smoking was supposed to stunt your growth."

"There are exceptions to every rule," Andrea retorted wryly.

❧

That evening, Uncle Bill picked us up sharply at 6:00. They must teach punctuality in accounting school, because, in all the years, we've never known him to be late. We bundled into his Explorer and set off for Chianti. Uncle Bill was sporting quite a tan and looked incredibly well-rested after his Caribbean jaunt.

"There's nothing like swaying palm trees in a warm sea breeze in March," he said, giving us the needle.

"Some guys have all the luck," I answered.

"By the time you two are my age, you'll be able to enjoy winters in the Caribbean too. In fact," he said with a twinkle in his eye, "you may not even have to wait quite as long."

"So, who's the chick you took with you, Uncle Bill?" I asked as Andrea jabbed me in the ribs.

"The *woman's* name is Karen. She's very nice, although, believe it or not, she's a lawyer. I never thought I'd see the day when I'd be dating a lawyer."

"Does she defend criminals?" I asked.

"Hardly," said Uncle Bill with a chuckle. "She actually handles patent applications."

"What's that?" asked Andrea.

"For example," explained Uncle Bill, "if you invent something and want to guarantee that nobody steals your invention, you make an application to the government for what's called proprietory rights. That means that the rights to your invention belong to you. She also handles copyrights for books and music and other things like that. The work itself isn't all that glamorous, but she does meet some pretty interesting people."

"Yourself included," said Andrea. We could almost feel our uncle blush in the semi-darkness of his car.

"Anyway," he said, "you'll probably meet her one day. We're going out for dinner Friday night with your Mom and Dad."

Andrea and I looked blank and pretended this was the first we had heard of it. Uncle Bill deftly steered the conversation to one of his favourite topics—hockey. I sat patiently while Andrea filled him in on the trials and tribulations of his beloved Calgary Flames who had upset Pittsburgh the week before, only to lose 6-0 to the Mighty Ducks. In short order, we arrived at Chianti and were shown to our table. We ordered cokes and spent a couple of minutes reading the menu. After the waiter took our food order, Uncle Bill took off his reading glasses and rubbed his hands together.

"I take it," he said, "this is not only a social outing. Normally, the proper protocol is to wait until after dinner to start discussing business. But since you guys have to be in bed early so you can be bright-eyed and bushy-tailed in the morning, we may as well get on to what you want to talk about. You both seem pretty excited."

Instead of saying anything, Andrea and I both reached into

our pockets, pulled out our paycheques and handed them to Uncle Bill.

"What should we do with this money?" asked Andrea.

"Yeah," I added. "Should we put this money in the bank, or what? If we simply cash these cheques, we're probably going to spend it all. Then we'll never be rich like you."

"Well," said Uncle Bill, "I sure am impressed! Congratulations on your first paycheques. You're throwing a whole lot at me all at once, though. So let's slow it down a bit. First of all, when we talked about saving and investing a couple of months ago, we used some examples that showed what you could accumulate if you put aside $200 a month. The thing is, though, *saving money for the long-term is not a whole lot of fun unless there are some rewards along the way.* If you guys were older and had families to support, you might need most of your paycheques to cover your regular monthly bills. Of course, as I explained earlier, from a very early age, you should still adopt the policy of *paying yourself first and setting aside, say, 10 per cent of your earnings for wealth accumulation.* But you're both still young and you should also have a bit of fun. My recommendation is that you save part of your paycheques for the long-term and hold back the rest so you can buy things. You must have some short-term goals that involve monetary requirements?"

"You're right," said Andrea. "I'd love to get a new pair of skis along with boots and poles next fall. But I'm looking at $300 to $400."

"Exactly my point," said Uncle Bill. "Let's assume you'll earn $210 a month. You could put aside one-third of that or $70 a month towards a *short-term savings program.* This way, you can reward yourself for earning money on an ongoing basis and it makes the whole idea of working a lot more fun. After five months, you'd have $350 and you can use that towards your skis, boots and what have you. Most of the rest of your money could go into a *long-term savings program.* What about you, Logan? What would you like?"

"Well," I answered, "I'll tell you if you promise not to laugh."

"Try me," said Uncle Bill.

"You know how Mom is allergic to most animals, and we've never been able to have a cat or a dog? But she's not allergic to birds. I have a friend who's got this neat parrot. It's an African Grey and the African Greys are the best talkers in the parrot kingdom. This guy has a vocabulary of over 40 words and phrases. It can say things like 'birds don't talk' and 'bird is the word'. Tommy Mulligan owns him. His father works for External Affairs and he's just been posted to Mozambique for a three-year period. The whole family is leaving at the end of the summer. Tommy told me he can't take his bird with him and he would sell Kiki, together with his cage and accessories, for $500 to someone who would give him a good home. I've checked in pet stores and to get a bird that *isn't* trained and *doesn't* talk along with a cage would probably cost anywhere from $1,000 to $1,500. I'd love to buy that bird. I think it would be an awesome pet. Up 'til now, I didn't really think a lot about it because I couldn't ask Mom and Dad for the money. But I suppose if I put aside $70 a month from now until the end of August, I'll have almost enough money to buy Kiki."

"If you're short $70 or $80," piped up Andrea, "I'll be able to help you because I won't need my short-term savings until October when I go out and buy my ski stuff."

"You'd really do that for me?" I asked, a bit shocked at my sister's generosity.

"Sure I would, brother dear," she said placing her hand on my arm. (We may have fought once in awhile when we were 'yo-ads', but, all in all, I think we got along pretty well.) "Who knows, maybe some day I'll need to borrow money from *you*."

"Okay," Uncle Bill interrupted. "You've set some reasonable short-term goals to shoot for. Now, what are you each going to do with the remaining $140?"

Andrea and I looked at each other and shrugged our shoulders.

"No idea?" asked Uncle Bill. "Okay, I'll tell you what I think, although you can decide on your own whether or not to take my advice. I really think you should each allow yourselves $10 a week, or $40 a month, to buy things; in other words, for general entertainment ... movies, concerts or the odd hamburger with your friends. Even if you're smart enough to avoid the costs and perils of smoking, drinking, and junk food, you still owe it to yourselves to enjoy *some* small indulgences, like a night out once a week or so. Fortunately, you guys aren't in a position where you actually have to contribute towards your family's cost of living. What I'm going to tell you next may sound a little calculating, but I don't mean it in a bad sort of way."

"What's that, Uncle Bill?" asked Andrea.

"To put it a bit harshly," he replied, "my advice is for you to *use your parents as long as possible.*"

"Use our parents? How so?" I asked.

"Well," replied Uncle Bill, "your parents aren't rich, but they can certainly afford to support you. They can give you room, board and clothing. In a year or two, you'll probably be borrowing the family car. So if they can afford to give you these things, you'd be foolish not to take advantage. There's an old saying I like to use: 'I'd rather be lucky than smart'. And both of you are lucky to be growing up in a country like Canada where most people have the basic amenities of a roof over their heads and enough food so they don't go to bed hungry. When I say *use* your parents I think you should also recognize that some day, you two will have the same obligation to your *own* children."

"Never," said Andrea, "I'm not going to have any kids."

"I don't know about that," said Uncle Bill. "You may change your mind. The point I'm trying to make though, is that if your parents look after you, and you in turn have kids down the line, it'll be *your* obligation to look after *them*. And so it goes from generation to generation. On the other hand, if you can function without receiving an entertainment allowance, then by your age, you owe it to yourselves *and your parents* to forgo this money. Knowing your Mom and Dad, they'll probably put aside whatever they were giving you before as allowances..."

"$10 a week," I piped in.

"...and hold it towards your education," continued Uncle Bill.

"I understand what you're saying," said Andrea. "And it

makes pretty good sense to me. I'll bet they'll be proud of us if we go to them tonight and tell them they no longer have to give us an allowance."

"I'm sure they will be," said Uncle Bill.

"But what about the extra $100 a month we're bringing home that we won't be spending right away or saving towards a short-term goal? What do we do with that?"

"Good question," replied Uncle Bill. "And I'll give you an answer, but you'll have to bear with me 'cause it'll take me a little while to get there. Ah," he continued, looking up. "Here's our food. Why don't we take a short break to eat this delicious pasta and I'll tell you what I think over dessert?" Without waiting for a response, Uncle Bill picked up his knife and fork and began to attack his plate.

❧

When we finished eating, Andrea and I ordered cheesecake for dessert while Uncle Bill contented himself with a cup of coffee.

"Okay," he said. "Now I'll tell you what I think you should do with your extra earnings of $100 a month. First of all, remember a couple of months ago, I gave you a broad outline of how the income tax structure works in this country?"

Andrea and I nodded.

"You'll recall, on the first $30,000 of income each year, the combined federal and provincial tax is about 25 per cent. Actually, when I told you this, I kind of over-simplified. The government recognizes that people in different circumstances should pay more or less tax than others. For example, if someone earns $30,000 and is single, that person should, in all fairness, pay more than someone who earns $30,000 and is supporting a spouse and children. Do you agree with that?"

"Seems okay. I guess that's right," said Andrea.

"Good. I'm glad we're in agreement," said Uncle Bill with a chuckle. "Now, the way the tax system works is that everyone gets a basic personal tax credit. And, without getting too technical, what this means in very simple language is that everyone has the opportunity to earn somewhere between $6,000 and $7,000 a year tax-free."

"What are you getting at?" I asked growing a bit impatient.

"Hang on, Logan," said Uncle Bill. "The points I'm going to try to make are really important for an overall understanding of how you should to invest your money. But you'll have to follow along with me one step at a time!"

"Sorry, Uncle Bill," I said apologetically.

"All right. Apology accepted. Now, let me continue."

Andrea and I nodded.

"Okay. Let's assume a person can earn 10 per cent on money that he or she is investing."

"Do the banks pay that much?" asked Andrea.

"Not today," replied Uncle Bill. "But again, you guys are putting the cart before the horse. Just let me explain in my own way and everything will become clear to you soon enough. Now, if you can earn 10 per cent on your money, but your tax rate is 25 per cent, what are you really earning?"

"Seven and a half per cent," said Andrea promptly.

"That's right. What if you were in a 40 per cent income tax bracket because you had income from a full-time job or business and then you *also* had some investments that were giving you a 10 per cent return over and above your earnings?"

"Then we'd only be able to keep six per cent," said Andrea.

"A real math whiz. You have a real math whiz for a sister, Logan," Uncle Bill said.

"I knew the answer too, Uncle Bill. She just got the words out faster, that's all."

"Yeah sure," said Andrea under her breath.

"Okay, cut the bickering, you guys, and let me explain my point," interrupted Uncle Bill. "What I've been getting at is really quite simple: *whenever you look at a rate of return on investment you always have to look at the after-tax amount.* In other words, 10 per cent might only mean seven and a half per cent in your pocket or, for top tax-bracket people, as little as four and a half or five per cent. The government takes the rest."

"I get you, Uncle Bill," I said. "Makes pretty good sense to me."

"Good," he replied. "Up until a couple of years ago, when bank interest rates were higher, say around seven to 10 per cent, I used to advise people who weren't taxable to simply keep their money in bank *term-deposits,* where they agree to invest their money at a certain rate of interest for a specific length of time. For example, a few years ago, my son, your cousin Jonathan, saved up $5,000 from a summer job while in second-year university. He asked me what to do with his money and I told him to simply buy a one-year term deposit. Because his total income was under $7,000, he wasn't in a position where he had to pay tax on his investment income. To put it in accountant's language, if I may be so bold, *his gross yield and his net yield were the same.*"

"So, since *we* won't be taxable on our

ADANAC BANK? I'D LIKE A LOAN TIL CHRISTMAS

TOY CO. LTD

WICKS

59

income as paper carriers, should we just put our money in the bank?" Andrea asked.

"If this were a few years ago, I would answer unequivocally 'yes'," said Uncle Bill. "But unfortunately times have changed and interest rates today are really very, very low. The government's current low-rate interest policy is great for anyone borrowing money but it isn't so terrific for people who have money to invest. On $100 a month, you'd be lucky to get anything more than four per cent and even if you don't have to pay tax, this isn't really an exciting yield. Granted, investing money with one of the major chartered banks is as risk-free as you can get. After all, if the Royal Bank, Bank of Montreal, or the Canadian Imperial Bank of Commerce collapse for example, you may as well flush our whole country down the proverbial toilet. But that's not likely to happen. If you decide you're absolutely dead-set against *any* risk whatsoever, by all means open up bank accounts, deposit your money and leave it there. At your age, though, I think you can afford to take a bit more risk because I think the rewards are well worthwhile. There's no reason why you shouldn't be able to earn 12 per cent on your money instead of three or four per cent. Also, for the next few years while your annual earnings are less than $7,000, you don't even have any income taxes to worry about."

"If we earn income, though," asked Andrea, "don't our parents lose us as tax deductions?"

"I see you've been doing some reading," said Uncle Bill proudly. "It's true you'll eventually no longer qualify as dependents, depending on how much you earn. But the tax benefits that the government gives to parents for children are really quite minimal. It's more tokenism than anything else. So, I really don't think you have to worry about hurting your Mom and Dad by earning income. You'll save them a lot more in weekly allowance than they would've gotten from the government by being able to take you on as dependents for tax purposes."

"So, Uncle Bill," I asked, "if we're not going to leave our extra $100 a month in a bank, what should we do?"

"In three words," he replied. "Growth Mutual Funds."

"Growth Mutual Funds. What's that?"

Uncle Bill took a deep breath and we could see he was again preparing to shift into lecture mode.

"What do you two know about the stock market?" he asked.

Andrea and I looked at each other, a bit embarrassed.

"Not a lot," said Andrea. "We know there's something about shares, that they trade and they go up and down, but, to be truthful, I don't even know what a 'share' is."

"Okay," said Uncle Bill. "Let me begin with the basics. When a business is started, whether it's a big business or a small business, the owners invest some of their money. Usually they *incorporate,* which means they set up a *corporation* which is a separate legal entity. What they get back in exchange for their investments is shares. *Shares are simply pieces of paper that bear evidence of a shareholder's investment.* In a simple example, let's assume a particular business is formed and there are going to be five equal owners." Uncle Bill looked at us to see if we were following. Andrea and I both nodded our heads.

"So, each investor puts up $200, for a total of $1,000. In exchange for the investments, the corporation, which, again, is a separate legal entity, issues 1,000 shares—200 to each investor." Andrea and I nodded again to indicate we were still on-side.

"Okay," said Uncle Bill. "Let's now look at one investor out of the five. He or she owns 200 shares out of a total of 1,000 shares. What does that mean?"

"I know," said Andrea. "It means that this person owns 20 per cent of the company."

"Exactly," said Uncle Bill. "This person has invested $200 out of a total of $1,000 and therefore owns 20 per cent of the company."

"So," I interjected. "Let's see if *I've* got this straight. If you have a share certificate, this means that you own a certain percentage of the company."

"That's right," said Uncle Bill. "If you take *your* number of shares and divide that by the *total* number of shares that the business has issued, you would then be able to calculate your percentage."

"But how do shares change in value? Like when they're traded on a stock exchange?" asked Andrea.

"I'll explain," said Uncle Bill. "Let's go back to the same example. Five people have each invested $200 for a total of $1,000. At that moment in time, when the company is just formed, what is each share worth?"

I shrugged my shoulders. "I suppose it's worth what these people put in. 200 shares at $200 per person. $1 for each."

"That's right. But now, what if the company starts to make money?"

"I get it!" I said excitedly as the light bulb went on. "If the company starts to make money, the shares become worth more."

"Right," said Uncle Bill. I could see he was very pleased with the way I was catching on.

"Andrea, what happens if the business loses money?"

"The shares will drop in value. They go down," said Andrea.

"Exactly," said Uncle Bill. "Now, in the case of a public company, such as one that is traded on the New York or the Toronto Stock Exchange, all we have is the same example I just gave you, but it involves thousands of investors and companies that haven't issued 1,000 shares but have issued, perhaps, *millions* of shares. So each individual share represents a very, very minute percentage interest in a big company."

"And if these companies make money," said Andrea, "their shares go up; if they lose, the shares go down."

"That's part of it, although the stock market is a more complex animal than an institution that simply reflects whether businesses are or aren't profitable. In a lot of cases, share prices will go up if it's expected in the foreseeable future that a business will start to make profits, or bigger profits, than before. Conversely, if a company releases some bad news, like they've lost a big contract and they've had to let a lot of employees go, the stock value will drop in anticipation of reduced earnings. There are several other factors that come into play as well."

"Such as?" I asked.

"For example, what if interest rates suddenly skyrocketed upwards? A lot of people who were investing in stocks might be inclined to sell these investments in order to put their money back in the banks."

"And with a whole bunch of sellers," said Andrea, "the market would drop."

"Exactly," exclaimed Uncle Bill. "On the other hand," he continued, "when interest rates are low, even novice investors such as yourselves, would be more inclined to put money into the stock market than into a bank."

"And with more people looking to buy stocks, the price goes up," I interjected.

"Yes," replied Uncle Bill. "What you guys have just 'discovered' is a very basic law of economics called *the law of supply and demand. If there's a high demand, price goes up. If supply outstrips demand, sellers have to lower their prices in order to make sales.*"

"But how does all this relate to mutual funds, Uncle Bill?" asked Andrea.

"I can see you're ready for Lesson Two. There are literally hundreds of stocks traded on stock exchanges in North America, and that doesn't even include the overseas markets. Stockbrokers are the people who actually do the buying and selling on behalf of their clients, whether the client is a rich individual, or the administrators of a pension fund, or even a small investor like yourselves. Stockbrokers make their money by charging fees or commissions on transactions they do for their clients." Uncle Bill paused to see if we were still following.

Andrea and I nodded our heads enthusiastically.

"The problem is that, in general, to get a decent price for some shares, one has to buy at least 100 shares at a time. This may not be a particular problem if you're speculating in an inexpensive speculative mining stock that sells for just pennies a share. But if you want to buy a 'blue chip security', such as Bell Canada or IBM, you might be looking at a single investment that costs anywhere between, say, $1,000 and $10,000. So, *to buy individual stocks you have to have a large amount of investment capital at your disposal.*"

"Makes sense to me, Uncle Bill," I said, urging him to carry on.

"Moreover," he continued, "you've no doubt heard the expression 'don't put all your eggs in one basket'?"

"Sure," said Andrea. "I guess what you're telling us is that, even if we had a few thousand dollars to invest, it wouldn't be wise to put all our money into one stock."

"Right again," said Uncle Bill patting her gently on the shoulder. "So here's where mutual funds come in. Mutual funds are administered by professional investment analysts. Their job is to study the various publicly-traded companies to try to determine, in advance, which companies are likely to do better than others. What these fund managers do, is they take a pool of money that they receive from many different people and then invest it in a whole bunch of different stocks. This spreads the risk around. In

HE SAYS HE'S MORE INTERESTED IN GROWTH MUTUAL FUNDS

other words, instead of owning 100 per cent of an investment in one company, you, as an individual, could own a very, very small percentage in literally *hundreds* of companies. If most of the investments held by the mutual fund go up, the value of *your* investment in the mutual fund *itself* goes up. Also, when you invest in a mutual fund, you get the buying power of many investors rolled together. Your commission, that is, the fee brokers charge for buying the stocks, would be lower and you'd also be buying professional advice. You wouldn't run the risk of dealing with a broker who might try to churn your portfolio..." Uncle Bill stopped at our look of confusion.

"Churn?"

"That's turning your holdings over and over. The broker buys and sells your shares more often than necessary to make more commissions. This is not really honest, but there are a few unscrupulous brokers who walk a fine line."

"So how do these guys who run the mutual funds make their money?" I asked a bit suspiciously.

"Good question," said Uncle Bill. "First of all, almost all of the mutual fund managers charge an ongoing administration fee, often around one per cent of the value of your investments on an annual basis. It's in their interests for you to be successful because the more your investments are worth, the higher their fee. Also, in most instances, there is what is called a 'front end load'."

"What's that?" asked Andrea.

"It's a commission charged on your initial investment every time you put money in. For example, if you invest $100, the mutual fund sales people and sales managers might take, say, five per cent. So you'd initially have only $95 working for you."

"You mean they take away our hard-earned cash?" I asked in dismay.

"They're providing a service," said Uncle Bill, "and they have to be paid for it. The thing is, if the mutual fund goes up in value, say, 15 per cent in one year, it doesn't take long for you to recover this commission. Sometimes there is a *'back-end load'* which applies if you want to sell and liquidate your investments into cash. My personal preference is to stay away from any fund that charges this kind of a fee. It can become too expensive since it's based on the future value of your investment. There's nothing really wrong, though, with paying four or five per cent up front each time you make an investment."

"Are all mutual funds set up to buy stocks that are supposed to go up in value?" I asked.

"No," said Uncle Bill. "There's a wide variety. Up 'til now, the type of fund that I've been describing to you is what is commonly called a *'growth fund'*. The object of the exercise is to invest money and hope that, on balance, the portfolio of company stocks held by the mutual fund grows in value. The more valuable it becomes, the more each mutual fund share or unit is worth. There are other mutual funds that also invest in the stock market, but the fund managers invest more in stocks that pay an ongoing income. In these cases, growth in value is of secondary interest."

"How do stocks pay income?" asked Andrea. "I thought they're only supposed to get more valuable over time—if you've invested in the right funds."

"Okay," said Uncle Bill. "I'll explain how that works, as well. Let's go back to the example I used before, where five investors get together and put up $200 each to start a business. Let's assume the business makes a $2,000 profit the first year. And just for illustration, let's assume the government takes 50 per cent of that away for income taxes."

"Boy, that's highway robbery," I said.

"I'm just giving you an example, Logan. In real life, corporate taxes aren't necessarily all that high, especially for small business. I'm sure the time will come when we'll get into a more detailed discussion of how the business tax system works. But for now, just please bear with me."

"Okay, Uncle Bill. The company has earned $2,000 and has paid $1,000 in taxes."

"Right, so what's it got left?"

"That's easy," said Andrea, "$1,000."

"Correct again," said Uncle Bill. "What do they do with that $1,000?"

Andrea and I looked at each other.

"Think about it for a minute."

"I suppose," said Andrea, "the owners could use the $1,000 to help the business get bigger."

"Bang on!" said Uncle Bill. "That's what a lot of businesses do. They use their after-tax profits for expansion. They buy equipment or inventory or sometimes they use their profits to even buy up other businesses. What else can the owners cause a business to do with its profits?"

"I know," I said, "the owners can take the money out and spend it."

"Good point," said Uncle Bill, "although, if owners take money for themselves out of the profits of a company, they have to pay personal income taxes on those withdrawals."

"So, the same profits are taxed twice?" asked Andrea.

"I think you should consider a career as a chartered accountant somewhere down the line," said Uncle Bill. "You're pretty good with these tax concepts."

"No, thanks," said Andrea. "I've always wanted to be an optometrist and that's what I'm going to do."

"I predict you'll be pretty good at running your own business some day, young lady," said Uncle Bill with a smile. "Now, when owners of a corporation take after-tax profits out of a business, these distributions are called *dividends* ..."

"So, that's what a dividend is," I interrupted. "I've often wondered. One of the cards in 'Monopoly' even talks about getting a dividend."

"That's right. *A dividend is a distribution out of a corporation's after-tax profits.* When the owners take this money, they have to report it as part of their personal incomes when they file their own income tax returns. But, as Andrea alluded just a moment ago, since dividends are distributions of profits that have already been taxed once, the owners are given what's called 'a dividend tax credit'. Now, I don't mean to make this too complicated for you. Suffice to say, dividends from Canadian companies are taxed more favourably than most other kinds of income. To put this in perspective, if a high-income investor is in a 50 per cent tax bracket, his or her tax on a Canadian dividend will only be about 37½ per cent. It's like getting a discount."

"I get what you're saying, Uncle Bill," I said. "But how does all this relate back to mutual funds?"

"I'll explain," he responded. "When companies make money and have paid their tax on their profits, they basically have the two choices that you, yourselves, figured out. The profits can either be used for business expansion, or they can be distributed to shareholders as dividends. Some companies, at one extreme, reinvest *all* their profits in expanding their businesses. At the other extreme, other companies distribute the vast majority of their profits as dividends to shareholders. Most businesses fall somewhere in the middle.

"So, if you were to select a single stock you could, on the one hand, choose a company that re-invests all its profits. If management makes good business decisions, you'll profit in the long-run from that company's *growth*. On the other hand, you could take your same investment and put your dollars into the shares of a second company that takes most of its profits and distributes them back to you as dividends. If the company is paying big dividends, they probably won't grow as quickly but you'll get *an ongoing income.*"

"So," said Andrea, "the choices are growth or income."

"Exactly," said Uncle Bill. "Often, retired people require ongoing income to meet their living expenses, while younger people, like yourselves, might be more interested in growth. Now, the mutual fund industry has recognized this and therefore some mutual funds that are 'equity-based'..."

"Equity-based?" I interrupted.

"Yes, that means they invest in stocks."

"Oh," I said.

"All right," continued Uncle Bill. "Some mutual funds that are equity-based invest with an emphasis on growth stocks and some invest to yield income."

"So, in our case, we'd be looking for growth. Wouldn't we, Uncle Bill?" asked Andrea.

"That's right. I'll just add one or two more points to complete the picture. Once you make a choice between growth and income, you can also select mutual funds based on geographical considerations."

"Which means?" I asked.

"Some funds sold in Canada invest only in Canadian securities; some invest in the U.S., some invest in the Pacific Rim countries—Japan, the Hong Kong market, etc.—and some invest overseas in Europe. Some mutual funds are blended and have diverse portfolios from all over the world. Some concentrate their investments in specific industries such as natural resources. There are also mutual funds that invest in bonds and mortgages."

"I know what a mortgage is, Uncle Bill. It's when you borrow money to buy a house."

"Or any piece of real estate for that matter," said Uncle Bill. "A mortgage is just the evidence on a piece of paper that a loan is secured by a particular piece of property. If the borrower doesn't pay, the lender can take away the property."

"Right," said Andrea. "But what is a bond?"

"A bond relates to a corporation or a government body, or even a municipality or school board, that borrows money and agrees to pay back at a later time. The people who lend the money get a piece of paper that summarizes their rights to receive both interest and the return of the original principal. When you invest in shares, you own a piece of a company. When you invest in a bond, you are lending money in exchange for interest. The rate of interest depends in part on the risk of the loan, and also the prevailing rates of interest that other loans bear—such as when you lend money to the bank."

"So, how does this stuff relate to mutual funds?" I asked.

"Consider this," Uncle Bill replied. "In the same way that most people don't have enough investment capital to buy a single stock, they also can't invest in individual bonds or mortgages. How would you feel, for example, if you were asked to lend $50,000 to one particular person to buy a house—if you had $50,000?"

"Um, not that great," I replied. "I suppose the borrower could lose his or her job and wouldn't be able to make the payments, or the house might burn down. No," I shook my head, "I really wouldn't want to invest in something like that."

"Well, this is the problem a mutual fund is designed to solve. In a mortgage-based mutual fund, for example, the fund managers take a pool of money they receive from many different people and spread the risk around. So, instead of owning 100 per cent of one mortgage, you might own a very, very small percentage of literally thousands of mortgages."

"So, I share the risk and the reward," Andrea said slowly.

Uncle Bill nodded. "I don't want to give you the impression you're always going to win. There's some element of risk in *any* mutual fund. For example, the whole stock market can collapse overnight. It's been known to happen. Also, even a mortgage fund could suffer a substantial loss if all the mortgages are secured by property in one province and its economy falls apart. But the point is, mutual funds are designed to spread out risk."

"I see," I responded. "Let's go over this again. For Andrea and me, investing in a fund geared towards paying out interest or dividends doesn't necessarily make sense at this time."

"True. What you need right now is a *growth* fund in which your money is invested in a *balanced* portfolio of stocks, probably primarily Canadian, perhaps some foreign, that is geared toward giving you *capital appreciation*. I don't think you should concentrate in any one industry. Many of the funds that have a good track-record for five or 10 years have averaged better than 12 or 14 per cent annual rate of return. And as long as your capital investment and growth in value remain in the fund...in other words, you don't cash out...the tax guys don't see what they call a disposition. As far as they're concerned, as long as you're not pocketing your earnings, the earnings don't count. It's only when you cash in all or part of your fund that you pay taxes. Remember, I showed you how money invested over a long-term period at 12 per cent can really become quite substantial. Well, 12 per cent annual growth is pretty darn good when inflation is around three per cent—and I'll tell you more about inflation some other time. Also, when one earns interest one has to pay tax. But if you can get your 12 per cent on a tax-deferred basis—as long as you don't sell– you're going to have quite a build-up over time. And here's something else you should consider."

We looked at Uncle Bill expectantly.

"For now, if you guys invest $100 a month, you'll benefit from something called *'dollar-cost averaging'*."

"Uncle Bill, I thought I told you I don't want to become an accountant," said Andrea with a hint of exasperation. "What's dollar-cost averaging?"

"Well, if you invest $100 a month, as I started to say," retorted Uncle Bill, "if the market drops at any point in time, you'll be able to buy *more shares in your mutual funds for the same money*. So, when the market goes back up again, you'll be in a position to make bigger profits. By having money going into an investment program on a regular and recurring basis, in the long-run you'll do a lot better than just trusting *luck,* which is what you have to do, if you make a single investment only. If you're lucky, you may make a one-time investment at the *bottom* of the market when prices are really low; but if you're unlucky, you could be investing at the *top*, when prices are over-inflated. So, an ongoing program makes a lot of sense. It'll give you the best returns and it's great for building up discipline."

"How do we pick a suitable fund?" I asked. "Do we get a list and just throw darts?"

"By track record, Logan," Uncle Bill laughed. "I've already said there's a number of growth funds out there, which have consistently averaged 12 to 14 per cent or better over five or 10-year periods."

"What about longer than 10 years?"

Uncle Bill shook his head. "It seems to me anything longer than 10 years doesn't really mean anything...it's just bragging." He smiled. "You see, any fund is only as good as its managers. And you have to expect some turn-over in personnel—especially over, say, 20 years."

I nodded. "Got it. Andrea and I really shouldn't concern ourselves about long track records."

"Exactly."

"But we should pay particular attention to three, five, and 10 year performances," said Andrea.

"Eventually, you might want to get into two or three different funds with different managers to hedge your bets. I'm going to introduce you to the fellow who looks after some of my investments. He represents three or four of the top funds and can give us some direction. His name is Jerry Laskowski. We'll make sure we pick funds that have reasonable charges—not more than four or five per cent and no back-end loads. There's only one little drawback which might create a potential problem."

"Uh, oh," Andrea said, "there's always a catch."

"Now don't be cynical, young lady. The only problem is the fact that you're both under-age and you can't own publicly-traded investments directly."

"So how do we get around that?" asked Andrea.

"You need an adult to act on your behalf and own your shares 'in trust'. It's really only a technicality. If you want, you can appoint either your Mom or Dad. Or I'll be happy to act on your behalf. We'll open up bank accounts, with me as trustee, in both your names so you can deposit your cheques... That's if it's okay with you and with your Mom and Dad. Then we'll set up mutual fund investment programs for both of you, with each monthly investment coming as an automatic withdrawal from your accounts a day to two following each payday."

"Sure, Uncle Bill. You're an accountant and although accountants are boring, Mom says they're generally quite trustworthy." I enjoyed giving my uncle the needle.

"Boring?" he said.

"Just joking, Uncle Bill. You're certainly far from boring."

"Okay, guys, it's time to go home. You've got another early day tomorrow. But I think we certainly have accomplished a lot tonight. You've got a game-plan for your paycheques: how much you're going to allot for ongoing spending; how much for short-term goals and how much into long-term savings. I'm really excited for the two of you. You've just started on your road towards financial security. You know, *if you never put aside anything more than $100 a month and you earn 12 per cent on your money, by the time you're my age you'll have almost $350,000 socked away.*"

"Together?" asked Andrea.

"Each of you," said Uncle Bill. *"And by the time you're 55 years old, you'd both be millionaires."*

"Wow. I can't believe that all adults aren't rich or at least comfortably well-off."

"The sad truth is that most people didn't get the right guidance when they were young. If you start early, you sure don't have to sacrifice a lot to get big rewards down the line."

"You know," said Andrea, "once or twice I've heard you use the expression 'I'd rather be lucky than smart'. We're pretty lucky to have you as our uncle."

It was kind of dark in the restaurant that evening but I could swear Uncle Bill actually blushed.

ANDREA'S STORY:
TURNING OUR HOBBIES INTO PROFITS

THAT YEAR, spring and summer passed very quickly. Our paper routes and studying for exams kept Logan and me pretty busy until the end of June. Then Logan managed to get a job for the summer mowing lawns, while I got lucky and landed a pretty cushy position as a mother's helper for a career mom with a six and a nine year old. Each day, I'd get to their house shortly before 8:00 after delivering my papers and then have breakfast with the kids while their mom and dad went out to work. The pay wasn't bad and the fact that I was busy all day didn't give me much opportunity to spend money. There was even a bonus two-week holiday with the family at their summer home on Buckhorn Lake. Of course, the holiday cost me a bit because I had to subcontract my paper route for that two-week period. By the time the summer ended, though, Logan and I had each socked away about $1,200: $600 from six months of deliveries for the Times-Herald and another $600 from our summer jobs.

We took Uncle Bill's advice and put these earnings into a growth mutual fund. Once a week, we would check the paper to see what we had and I'm proud to say that, by September, we had already earned about $100 in accumulated growth. So Logan and I had gone from zero to a net worth of $1,300 each in just six short months! To make things even better, we had more than ample spending money and Mom and Dad were really pleased they no longer had to give us allowances. Also, by summer's end, Logan was able to buy his friend's parrot (with bird cage) for $500 and I was just a little bit shy of the new ski equipment I had picked out.

When I got back from my two weeks with those people at their cottage, I was amazed at the change in my brother. Being outside mowing lawns had improved his colour (and complexion) significantly and he was fairly rippling with muscles. What I found most amusing, though, was how he doted on his African Grey, Kiki. It seems that his friend's father was transferred a bit earlier than anticipated and Logan got the bird at the beginning of August instead of in September as originally planned.

Kiki's vocabulary was no less than awesome, although it was more than a bit weird to listen to an animal who tells you that 'birds don't talk'. In just a couple of short weeks, Kiki learned the words 'Logan rules', and would repeat this little litany several times a day to the point that it drove the rest of us nuts. Logan made sure that Kiki's wings were clipped so he couldn't fly away and get lost but Kiki didn't seem to mind. He spent a lot of time riding on my brother's shoulder and would eat out of virtually anybody's hand. Unfortunately, Kiki was a bit deficient in the toilet-training department and Mom grumbled a bit about the additional laundry loads. Logan must have had a pretty good sense of self-preservation though, because he was smart enough to keep Kiki off Mom's carpets.

As I write this, Kiki is still alive and well and hasn't aged a bit over the last 20 years. Then again, Logan says parrots often live for a hundred years or more. Leave it to my brother to get the most out of a $500 investment!

If truth be told, though, Logan and I were both a bit tired by the time Labour Day rolled around and we were on the verge of starting another school year—our last in high school! Getting up early to deliver papers and then holding a summer job was starting to take its toll. But we were already hooked on the idea of earning money for both spending and investment, and we weren't about to quit.

One night, I worked up the courage to tell Logan I was feeling a bit out of sorts and the minute I finished speaking I was amazed at the extent of his wide grin.

"I feel the same way, Sis," he said. "There's got to be a better way to make money than delivering papers."

"Let's ask Uncle Bill," I suggested. "He sure hasn't steered us wrong so far."

"Oh, is he back in town?" Logan asked.

"I overheard Mom tell Dad that he'll be back from his Alaska cruise the day after tomorrow. So I'm sure we'll see him sometime this week. I'll leave a message on his answering machine to call us as soon as he's got some free time."

"I'm sure he's going to want to meet Kiki."

"You and your bird," I said shaking my head. "I suppose, in the long-run, that bird will make you rich because you'll never feel the need to get married and have a family."

"Very funny, Sis," Logan replied. "There are still a few things that Kiki can't do...."

❧

The following Sunday was one of the most glorious Indian Summer days imaginable. Uncle Bill had called on Friday night and invited us to visit him on the Sunday afternoon. He suggested we could go for a swim in the pool at his condo complex and then we could all join up with Mom and Dad for a nice dinner. I forgot to mention that I had just gotten my learner's permit that summer so I was able to drive us over to Uncle Bill's place with Mom navigating in the front passenger seat and Logan cowering and making snide remarks in the back.

Logan was a bit bummed because Mom wouldn't let him bring Kiki over to Uncle Bill's house. To keep the peace, she finally had to promise to invite Uncle Bill over for coffee that night after dinner.

Logan and I took turns changing into swimsuits in Uncle Bill's spare bedroom and, armed with a pitcher of lemonade, the three of us went down to the pool. We swam for awhile, lay in the grass soaking up some rays, and finally joined our uncle who was sitting under a patio umbrella reading some book called *'The Wealthy Procrastinator'*.

"Whatcha reading, Uncle Bill?" I asked.

"A novel actually. It's a story about this couple who are more or less broke at age 45 and yet are able to retire as millionaires only 20 years later. The philosophy in this book ties in very nicely with my own—slow and steady; no get-rich-quick schemes—just a regular savings program. I was just thinking how much better off you guys are having started at 15 instead of 45."

"Well, Uncle Bill," piped in Logan, "we kind of wanted to talk to you about that. We're both enjoying earning money and watching our savings grow but, to be honest, we're finding the paper route work somewhat tedious to say the least."

"Such big words," I said in mock horror. "When did you start reading?"

Logan ignored my comment—a sign of his emerging maturity. "It's tough work, Uncle Bill, and to tell the truth it's not particularly interesting or challenging."

Uncle Bill leaned back, put his hands behind his head and plopped his legs on the table. "I'm not surprised at your conclusion. In fact, I was sort of waiting for this reaction and I frankly expected it even before summer started. Remember my motto, 'work smart, not hard'?"

Logan and I nodded.

"Well, perhaps now you're in a better position to understand what I mean. There's got to be a better way for you to earn money than getting up at 5:30 or 6:00 in the morning to deliver newspapers. Now, there are the old standbys. You can try and get a job at Woolco after school or on weekends or working at McDonald's or Wendy's. You might even find something as a bus-person in a restaurant which will pay you minimum wage and maybe even some tips. But all of these jobs involve long shifts that are going to take up a number of evenings a week and your weekends. And you're competing against umpteen zillion other teenagers who are looking at the same job

opportunities. So, whether you're working from 7:00 to 8:00 in the morning or from 8:00 to 11:00 at night, you're still working hard, not smart."

"You're right, Uncle Bill. There's gotta be something better. But what is it?"

"My first bit of advice," he replied, "is to stay away from McJobs."

"McJobs?" Logan and I asked in unison.

"Yes, low-pay, low-prestige, low-benefit, no-future jobs in the service industry."

"Wow, that was well put," I said.

"Actually," said Uncle Bill, "I wish I could take the credit for that description, but it isn't mine. A fellow named Douglas Coupland wrote a book called 'Generation X' that came out in the early '90s and he seems to have coined that term."

"But what choice is there?" Logan wailed.

"Well, if you were a night owl, I understand from my bank manager that the Canadian Imperial Bank of Commerce hires students to do data input at night and they pay between $8 and $12 an hour."

"But what about our homework and our sleep?" I asked.

"It's a thought, so I just decided to mention it. It's not a recommendation."

"So what should we do, Uncle Bill?" I asked.

"Ah, ha," he said. "I've got something to show you." He reached down and pulled a book from the folds of his towel. He held it up for us to see the title: 'Better than a Lemonade Stand— Small Business Ideas for Kids by 15 year old Daryl Bernstein'.

"What's that, Uncle Bill?" Logan asked

"What does it look like? It's a book. I happened to pick it up in the Vancouver Airport while waiting for my plane back to Ottawa last week. It's really neat. There are actually 51 different business ideas for kids that are certainly, for the most part, far more interesting and entrepreneurial than the standard McJobs."

"Lemme see it," said Logan, reaching out his hand.

"Not so fast," said Uncle Bill. "When I went through it, I spotted two different ideas, one for you and one for Andrea,

80

that I think would be just perfect. Please indulge me. I'd like to see whether you guys can come up with these ideas independently without looking at the book."

"We're not mind-readers," I said, somewhat exasperated.

"You don't have to be a mind-reader, but let's make this into a little game. Let me ask you each a couple of questions. If I can get your thinking going in the right direction, I'll bet you'll come up with your *own* ideas."

Logan and I gave each other a look that said 'what the heck, let's indulge the old guy'.

"Who wants to start?" asked Uncle Bill.

"Ladies first," I said. "But believe me, I have no idea where to start."

"I told you I'd help you," replied Uncle Bill.

"Oh well," I thought, "maybe this will be fun after all."

"Okay," said Uncle Bill. "What are you good at in school?"

"Everything," I answered.

"What modesty," interjected Logan.

"All right," said Uncle Bill. "What do you especially like?"

"Science, computers, and math."

"Do you think you can earn any money out of your interest in science?"

I thought for a minute before answering. "Not now, Uncle Bill. But you do know I want to be an optometrist. I'll need science for that."

"That's true," said Uncle Bill. "But you're right. You probably can't use your knowledge or love of science to earn money right now. What about math?"

"I'm good at math and I suppose I could tutor other kids, but there are a couple drawbacks."

"And what might they be?" Uncle Bill asked.

"First, most kids don't have a lot of money and also the teachers at my school are quite willing to stay after class and help out. Also, any tutoring work would be quite sporadic and would be concentrated around exam time. So, I don't think my math skills are the answer."

"What's left?" asked Uncle Bill.

"Computers, I guess," I replied. "I've always been really good at learning software programs, even from when I was a little girl and Dad bought me an Apple IIC. I've learned WordPerfect, spreadsheet programs and am pretty good with graphics packages too."

"So...," said Uncle Bill.

"Are you suggesting I can teach computer programs to others?"

He smiled in reply.

"I never thought of that," I said. "What do you think I can make?"

"No reason you can't earn $10 an hour. If you teach a couple of people at the same time and charge $7.50 each, that's $15 an hour. Once you get good, you might even be able to give instruction for companies and make a lot more."

"How do I go about advertising, though?"

"Use your imagination. What do you think?"

"I suppose I can use my own desk-top printing program at home to produce a flyer. I know the people at Bits n' Bytes near the house from whom I get most of my software. Maybe they'll distribute my flyers to their customers. I can also put an ad on our community centre bulletin board."

"Now you're on the right track," said Uncle Bill.

"This sure is a better idea than delivering newspapers, isn't it? What do you think I can earn?"

"Probably double what you're earning now. $10 an hour, 10 hours a week, 40 hours a month. You should be good for at least $400 each and every month. And you'll be able to do your teaching when you want, which probably isn't going to be at 5:30 in the morning."

"So that's what you mean by working smart, not hard," I said, as the light bulb suddenly went on.

"That's right. Some day, you're probably going to want to open up your own optometry practice. The skills you get in running a business today will certainly stand you in good stead down the line. For the time being, you might want to keep your paper route with the Times-Herald until you've built up some clientele. By the way, always make sure after you finish teaching a 'client' that you get some good references and referrals."

"I'll even get some business cards printed up," I said. "I'll need a catchy name though, for my little venture."

"How about Andrea Lavery, Computer Consultant—her bark is worse than her byte," interjected Logan.

Uncle Bill and I both laughed.

"I'm sure you'll think of something," said Uncle Bill. "Okay, Logan, now it's your turn."

"Can't I take a look at the book?" Logan asked hopefully.

"Nope," said Uncle Bill. "You've gotta play the game the same way your sister did. What do you like to do?"

"If you're talking about school, to be honest, there isn't a whole lot that turns my crank. I mean, I do okay, but I'm not like Miss Brilliance over here."

"So you don't feel you have any school-related skills that are marketable?" asked Uncle Bill.

"Not really," replied Logan.

"All right then," said Uncle Bill, "what are your hobbies?"

"Girls, sports, girls, roller blading, girls and his bird," I said.

"The famous Kiki," said Uncle Bill. "Is it true he talks a blue streak all the time?"

"You bet," replied Logan enthusiastically. "Sometimes I can teach him a new word or phrase in a matter of a few hours. He's the greatest. I've even joined the Ottawa Bird Club. They have meetings once a month and someone always brings in a parrot for show and tell. Kiki is a fabulous pet..."

"If only he were toilet-trained," I said a bit disgustedly. "The other day..."

"That was an accident," said Logan. "I can always tell when he's gotta go and I take him back to his perch or cage."

"Let's stick to this hobby of yours," said Uncle Bill. "What's the one part about having a parrot that you don't really enjoy?"

Logan thought for a moment. "I guess it's cleaning his cage once a week. I change the paper at the bottom every day, but once a week, I've got to give that cage a good cleaning. I wash it down and use disinfectant. If I don't, it gets to be pretty gross."

"So," said Uncle Bill, "do you think other people might feel the way you do about cage-cleaning?"

"Are you suggesting I can go into business cleaning parrot cages? I never thought of that," said Logan. "But you're right. There are at least a dozen members of the Ottawa Bird Club who live in this general area and some of them have three or four birds. I'll bet I could make $7.50 a cage, and Jim at Pet Haven down the street from us would probably let me distribute some flyers to people who buy birds from him. Andrea, would you do up a flyer for me on the computer, please?"

"For a small fee," I said jokingly.

"Wow," continued Logan, "if I could get contracts to clean just 10 cages a week, that's $75 a week, $300 a month and I could probably make some extra money by arranging to go into people's homes to feed and play with their birds when they're on holidays. Parrots require a good deal of attention, you know. They're like kids. Did you know that the average parrot has the intelligence of a five year old?"

"If he doesn't stop with his damn birds, I'm going to puke," I said disgustedly. "That's all he ever talks about."

"What about you and your computers?" asked Logan, getting on the defensive.

"Let's cut out the fighting, you guys," said Uncle Bill. "We've really made some good progress here. It's interesting that both of your ideas are in this book *'Better than a Lemonade Stand'* and you guys were able to come up with them independently."

"Can we borrow the book and read it?" I asked.

"Sure," said Uncle Bill. "Maybe some of your friends at school can get some ideas from it too, as long as they promise not to compete with you. But you see how easy it really is to become entrepreneurial and do something a little different than jostle with everybody else for the low-paying jobs at McDonald's, 7-Eleven, and the like. *All you have to do is ask yourself what you're good at and how your interests and skills can be translated into earning money.*"

"It won't be too long," said Logan, "before we'll be taking *you* out to dinner and picking up the tab."

Uncle Bill chuckled. "It's hot. I think I'll jump back into the pool. You guys want to join me?"

"Last one in's a rotten egg," I said.

Chapter Seven

January 1996

Logan's Story:
Decisions, Decisions, Decisions

THAT FALL SEMESTER flew by in the wink of an eye. Andrea really buckled down at school because she was gunning for a scholarship to university the next year. Not to be out-shone by my older sister, I put in my fair share of time hitting the books. We were still able to pursue our business ventures with a vengeance, though and, to be honest, our social lives didn't suffer either. Uncle Bill was right. *To get ahead as a 'yo-ad', you have to either give up sleep or sitcoms.*

By October, we were both able to resign our paper routes and we welcomed the opportunity to get an extra hour's sleep in the morning. By forgoing watching TV, I was able to build up a neat little business cleaning bird cages while Andrea did fantastically well teaching computer software. Business was even better than either one of us had imagined. We were each averaging about $400 a month, out of which we were spending $40, keeping $60 aside for Christmas gifts and plowing $300 into mutual funds.

By the end of the year, our investment capital was over $2,500—each. I earned a couple of hundred dollars extra by making some simple wooden bird toys with my Dad over several weekends, while Andrea discovered she could make extra money buying popular software packages from wholesalers and re-selling them to her clients at a price just a bit lower than the stores were charging. I'll never forget how excited she was when she discovered she could get 10 copies of WordPerfect 7.1 from a local distributor for about 60 per cent of what they sold for in stores. By selling them at 90 per cent of their retail value, she picked up several hundred additional dollars.

Just after the holiday season ended, though, Andrea and I suddenly came face to face with a pretty harsh reality—our nice, sheltered high school existence was rapidly coming to a close! Our teachers began to emphasize that we were approaching a day of reckoning. We would have to make choices for jobs, careers, and further education. I envied Andrea because, from an early age, she seemed to know exactly what she wanted. Having inherited Mom's poor eyesight, she developed an interest in optometry early on. Fortunately, she was able to wear contact lenses most of the time, because, if the truth be told, she didn't look all that great with coke bottles suspended from her nose. For her, the path was clear: a science degree (hopefully) followed by admission into the optometry program at the University of Waterloo.

I was the one with the problem. I was starting to face up to the fact that I really didn't want to go to an academic degree-oriented university. I liked the idea of going into my own business selling some interesting product and I really wondered whether I needed a full-blown four-year program to reach my objective. But I was afraid to disappoint Mom and Dad, both of whom were university graduates.

One Friday afternoon, on the way home from school, I finally blurted out to Andrea my concern that I didn't want to disappoint the family by not going on to Carleton or Ottawa U, which was what they seemed to expect.

"Why don't we get together with Uncle Bill?" suggested Andrea. "Maybe he'll have some good ideas."

It seemed the logical thing to do, so I called Uncle Bill that evening and he offered to buy me brunch the next Sunday morning at Nate's Deli. I asked if Andrea could come too and insisted it would be our treat. Uncle Bill laughed and agreed to a compromise. We'd go dutch.

❧

Sunday morning, the three of us dined like kings on Montreal bagels covered with creamed cheese and smoked salmon. It was great to be young and active and not have to worry about what or how much we ate. Today, I've got to work at keeping trim and I often remember what Mom used to say: "Youth is wasted on the young." It pissed me off back then, but I can see now she was right!

"So, what's on your mind, Logan?" asked Uncle Bill as he sipped thoughtfully on his third cup of coffee.

"It just dawned on me this week," I replied, "that we're into our last six months of high school and I really don't want to go to university. In fact, I'm not 100 per cent sure what I'd like to do...Damn, I wish I was more like Andrea. At least she knows what she wants."

"Now, don't get upset, Logan," said Uncle Bill, putting his arm on my shoulder. "I know you're coming to an important crossroads, but it isn't really a life or death decision. You'll probably change careers several times during the course of your life."

"All I know is I'd really like to be my own boss. While this cage-cleaning work is not something I'd want to do forever, I like making my own hours, charging what I think is fair, and doing things on my own. I may not want to go to university full-time, but I really would be interested in taking a marketing diploma course at Elgin College. I'm really afraid, though, that Mom and Dad are going to have a cow if I tell them."

"Don't sell your parents short," said Uncle Bill. "Let me tell you a story. You know your cousin Ron, my oldest son?"

"Sure," I said.

"About 12 or 13 years ago when he was 16, your Aunt Helen and I took the kids to Hawaii for the first time. None of the kids had ever been in an airplane before. When we boarded this enormous 747, I had never seen Ron so excited. It was almost like he'd found religion. He got a stewardess to give him a complete tour of the plane and even managed to visit the cockpit. He was in Grade 11 at the time.

"A couple of months later, your aunt and I were sitting in the living room one night. I was reading and she was doing needlepoint and Ron came in and asked if he could talk to us. We told him to sit down and he blurted out he had decided he didn't want to go to an academic university. Instead, he had made the decision he wanted to be a pilot and he wanted to apply to the aviation school at Mount Royal College in Calgary.

"Your aunt and I looked at each other, shrugged our shoulders, smiled at him, and said 'go for it'.

"He asked, 'You mean you're not mad?' and your aunt said, 'Of course, we're not mad. We know you, and we know that although you have the talent to go to university, that really isn't what would turn you on. If you want to be a pilot, why shouldn't you do what you want?' I could see the weight of the world drop off Ron's shoulders when he received our blessing.

"Now, if you want to take a diploma in marketing instead of a degree program, I'm sure your Mom and Dad will understand. You can always change your mind later on, if and when you decide you want to go on with a more academically-oriented education—especially if you've got some money saved up. Don't be afraid. Talk to your parents and tell them what you'd like to do."

"Actually," I said, "I do have an idea and I'll share it with you if you promise not to laugh. I haven't even told Andrea yet."

"Fire away," said Uncle Bill.

"I've got a friend at school, Rene Marleau, whose older brother works with this company selling kitchen knives."

"Kitchen knives?" Andrea gasped incredulously.

"Yes, kitchen knives," I said. "In fact, he's even given me a brochure." I reached into the pocket of my jacket and pulled out a glossy pamphlet which I slapped down on the table. "Now these knives are incredibly good. They're even better than the German Shickels."

"What store do you buy them at?" Uncle Bill asked. "Actually, I can use a set of knives."

"That's the whole point," I said excitedly. "They're not sold in stores and not really sold door-to-door either. What you do is you make your contacts with friends, neighbours, relatives, and so on and the company teaches you how to do a demonstration. At the end of every demonstration, you ask the customers, whether they buy or not, to give you a list of five other people to whom you can show the product. Then, you follow up the new leads. And they really are fantastic knives. The only thing is, they're pretty expensive. It's just under $1,000 for this complete set over here." I pointed to show my uncle the display in the pamphlet.

"It sounds like a lot," I continued, "but these knives are guaranteed for life. The company that's selling them has been operating in the U.S. for many years and they're just now starting to expand into Canada. Their commission structure is as high as 30 per cent if you attain a reasonable sales volume. Rene told me his brother earned over $10,000 from May through August during his summer holiday from university. The district manager earned over $100,000 and he's just 24 years old. I really would like to get on with this company and see how much I enjoy sales. In fact, Rene told me his brother would get me an interview as soon as I wanted it. I'm pretty sure I could land the job."

"Sounds pretty interesting to me," said Uncle Bill. "I'm not sure you're going to want to sell knives for your whole life, but at least you'll learn something about marketing first-hand. And, by the way, if these knives are as good as you say they are, I'll be your first customer."

"So you really don't think Mom and Dad are going to give me a whole lot of grief?" I asked.

"I don't think so, Logan. Try. Talk to them. Tell them how you feel and I'm sure everything will be okay."

I relaxed visibly and decided to celebrate by ordering strawberry cheesecake.

"While you're here, Uncle Bill," said Andrea, "there are a couple of things that I'd like to ask, if you don't mind."

"Fire away."

"Well, I know what I want to do and I shouldn't have any trouble getting into the science program in virtually any university in Canada. But I'm not sure whether I'm better off staying here in Ottawa or going away to college. What are your thoughts?"

"That's a difficult question," Uncle Bill replied. "There are advantages and disadvantages to both alternatives. The major advantage of going away is that a young person really learns how to live on his or her own. I think you'd make closer friends and really get to understand human nature better than if you stay within the cocoon of your own family. As long as you take your education seriously, you'd have a pretty good blend of structure on the one hand and freedom on the other.

"When I was growing up, I lived in Montreal and because McGill University was in my own backyard, so to speak, I stayed at home. Looking back, I think I missed quite a bit because, for me, university wasn't a lot more than an extension of high school. I worked hard at my classes, did well in school, but I really didn't make many close friends. When your cousins, Jonathan and Cheryl, reached university age, I strongly recommended they *not* go to the University of Calgary and that they go out of town instead.

"There were a couple of other factors, though. Number one, their mother and I were getting divorced and I think it was a lot less traumatic for them to be away. Secondly, and perhaps more important, your Aunt Helen and I could afford to pay for their education. I think a lot of young people find it oppressive to graduate from college and find themselves many thousands of dollars in the hole because of student loans. As it is, living at home, but having to pay for your own books and tuition, can be enough of a strain on your budget. Remember, many kids aren't as innovative as you are in their ability to earn money and invest it."

"Also," I piped in, "most of them don't have an Uncle Bill to show them the way." It was neat to see our uncle blush.

"Anyway," Uncle Bill continued, "if you live in a city such as Ottawa, where there are excellent institutions of higher learning, I think, today, it's probably a good idea for you to stay at home and take advantage of what you've got. This is as long as your home life is reasonably okay—which yours is. If *I* had to do it all over again, I might not have left Montreal at the time, but I sure would have made a greater effort to get involved in student activities. If you stay here, find some clubs you enjoy and try to make a few good friends. You'll be going out of town anyway, Andrea, at some point, when you enter optometry school. Your Mom was telling me Waterloo is the only English-speaking

92

optometry school in the country. You've got your work cut out for you over the next four years just to get in. She also told me they only take 60 students out of over 500 applicants each year."

"I'll get in, Uncle Bill. You leave that to me. I'll also save enough money over the next four years so that the years at Waterloo won't be a financial problem. If I'm still teaching computers, I suppose I can do that there as well as here. The only thing is, what do you think I should look at in the summer time? I'm not sure I can get enough hours to make computer-teaching viable as a full-time occupation. I probably could get a job in a computer store, but I'd be looking at minimum wage. Eventually, I'd like to own my own optometry practice—maybe not initially—but once I got to be really good at what I'm doing. I'm much more interested in having a little business rather than a job."

"There are a lot of opportunities if you look for them. All you have to do is keep your eyes open. Let me show you something that I clipped out of the Ottawa Citizen—the competitor to the Times-Herald that gave you your start. Take a minute and read this article."

Students take plunge

By David Scanlan
(Ottawa Citizen)

Andrew Lay caught the student-business bug early.

Eight years ago, when he was just 14, Lay saved $3,000 from his paper route to invest in the hot dog cart business.

He's been a fixture near Sparks and Banks Streets in Ottawa every summer since, doling out hot dogs, Italian sausages and drinks to the public-service lunchtime set.

The University of Ottawa student has tried restaurant jobs, a common recourse for many students trying to make money. But he always comes back to his hot dog cart, where he's the chef, accountant, buyer and marketing manager all at once.

"(When you're working for someone else) they're making a profit off you as opposed to you making a profit for yourself," says Lay, who has earned up to $10,000 in past summers.

"I don't even think of it as work."

93

For the last six summers, Lay has relied on loans from the Ontario government's student-venture program to buy supplies, his vendor's licence and other necessities.

Lay has already started his summer work, but many students are shying away from starting their own businesses. The recession seems to be intimidating many college and university students from taking the entrepreneurial plunge.

The number of students getting summer business loans from the Ontario government has dropped 43 per cent in the last five years. As recently as 1988, 1,195 students were granted loans. Just 683 students got loans last summer.

"People aren't as willing to take the risk in hard times," explains Narvin Singh, a spokesman for the loans program in Toronto. The government program offers loans of up to $3,000 for students returning to school in the fall. They are granted by the Royal Bank but guaranteed by the province and are interest-free until September30, after which interest is charged at the prime lending rate plus one percentage point. Singh says the loan-applications process has had an acceptance rate of nearly 90 percent in recent years.

The businesses tend to rely on outdoor and seasonal work, including house-painting, window-washing, landscaping and gardening, selling hot dogs and ice cream—and the old standby, lemonade stands. Other summer businesses in the past have included carpet-cleaning, catering, video rentals and doll-making.

The students who do take the risk tend to prosper. Last summer, the 683 businesses started under the student-venture program in Ontario had average revenues of $27,000 and profits for the entrepreneurs averaged $5,600.

Some tips for student entrepreneurs:

■ Be prepared to work long days. Ten- to 14-hour days are not uncommon when you're starting up a business.

■ Stick to a single niche or geographic area. Concentrate on one neighbourhood at a time.

■ Keep costs down. If you're using flyers to promote your business, try to get them done as cheaply as possible. Consider telemarketing.

■ Exploit your "starving-student" status. People like to help out eager students. Hire other students.

"Wow," said Andrea after she finished reading. "What a fabulous concept. Give me a bit of time and I'll bet you I can come up with something. It may not be a hot dog stand, but I'll make it successful...if it kills me."

"I'm sure you won't have to go that far," said Uncle Bill dryly. "I remember reading another article a while back about a young fellow from Victoria who at the age of 11 was selling desktop aquariums at a booth at the Calgary Stampede. He was written-up by the media as the Stampede's youngest entrepreneur. There is also a chain of restaurants in Western Canada called 'Joey's Only Seafood' that was started by an 18-year- old. There's no law that says kids today have to take McJobs. *There are choices—but you've got to be innovative.*"

"Uncle Bill?" I asked. "What actually went wrong in our society? We've discussed this a bit in school and I've talked to my friends about it. It seems we are the first generation that won't necessarily have more than our parents. Do you think *we'll* grow up to have nice homes, winter vacations, two cars, and so on? It seems pretty tough out there."

"I can tell you what *I* think went wrong," said Uncle Bill. "But I'm not sure I can fix it. The good news, though, is as I just said, there's room for entrepreneurs and innovative thinkers. I get great enjoyment out of helping the two of you because you're willing to use your minds and think of alternatives rather than taking the easy way out and scrounging for minimum-wage jobs. Unfortunately, I don't think I can necessarily help everybody. *What's really important is that, if a young person has a good idea and he or she talks it over with someone, whether it's an uncle like myself or a parent or a teacher at school, the best thing the adult can do is to provide some positive moral support.* Sometimes it may be healthy to play devil's advocate. But *kids should be taught how to do things—not 'don't do it—it won't work'.* If our society is to prosper into the 21st Century, we need a fresh approach."

"I agree with you," I said. "And believe me, Andrea and I are very grateful for what you've done. But what *did* go wrong? Do you mind taking a few minutes and explaining?"

"I can try. But first, let me just take a short trip to the washroom. At my age, I should know better than to have four cups of coffee with breakfast."

"Four cups?" said Andrea. "You've only had three."

"Yes, but I'll have a fourth when I get back."

CHAPTER EIGHT

ANDREA'S STORY: PARADISE LOST
(WITH APOLOGIES TO THE ENGLISH POET JOHN MILTON)

WHEN UNCLE BILL RETURNED from the washroom, true to his word, he signalled the waitress for another cup of coffee, added a bit of milk, took a swallow and jumped into lecture mode.

"You guys want to know what went wrong in our society, so I'll tell you what the problem is. Now, I'm not sure everybody would agree with me and I want to preface my comments by telling you this is really *my* opinion and it isn't necessarily shared by everyone." Uncle Bill paused, and Logan and I nodded our heads.

"To know what went wrong," continued Uncle Bill, "we really have to go all the way back to the 1950s, a few years after World War II ended. All of a sudden, the technology that had gone into the war-time effort was channelled into peace-time entrepreneurial activity. For example, automobiles became sleeker and more reliable; television, which had been invented before World War II, became commercially viable. There was an incredible number of inventions for which manufacturing started right here in North America. We had very little unemployment in those days as people in this country and the U.S. went to work building things—making things for their own consumption. Houses started to go up all over. The word 'suburbia' never existed before World War II, but the suburbs sure became a fact of life in the '50s and '60s. It got so that it became every North American's God-given right to own a house, a car, a washing machine, a clothes dryer, a television set and so on.

"The people who were working making things kept getting raises in pay year after year and the raises in pay came to be expected, as well. I suppose, although I've never tried to verify this, for many years, the powers that ran big business in North America didn't begrudge their workers increases in income because their businesses were prospering and *they too* were doing very well financially. Actually, now that I think about it, even if businesses *did* begrudge their workers money, the labour unions were there to protect them.

"But in the 1970s, the decade before you were born, North America started to experience some pretty significant inflation. Now I don't want to get side-tracked with a whole long discussion of what inflation is all about—not at this time anyway—although I'll be happy to talk to you about it some other time. Suffice to say, inflation is when prices go up and usually when prices go up, salaries go up as well."

"It makes sense to me," I said. "If the cost of living goes up, you're going to ask your boss for a raise."

"That's right," said Uncle Bill, "and back then, even if *you* didn't ask your boss for a raise, your union did it for you. All quite justified. In the meantime, other countries around the world started to evolve economically, and by the end of the 1970s, it suddenly became clear that North American-made goods had become too expensive relative to goods made in other countries. You see, higher wages gave our people more money to spend. They bid the price of goods up by going on buying sprees. But higher wage costs also meant that goods cost more to buy. So workers asked for even more money. This created an inflationary spiral. Before we knew it, our labour costs priced us right out of world markets!"

"I get it," I said. "If the Japanese, say, had a lower labour cost, they could afford to make the same things we were making here, but they were able to charge less for them."

"Exactly. And the whole process filtered right through the entire manufacturing system."

"What do you mean?" I asked.

"Well," said Uncle Bill, "let's assume there are, just for simplicity, 100 different components to making up a TV set. If the labour cost to make *all* 100 components is cheaper in Japan, for example, the entire television set is going to be *way* cheaper, even when we consider the cost of shipping it to North America."

"Yes," I said, "that makes sense."

"Okay," continued Uncle Bill. "We reached a point where it became pretty expensive to manufacture things here in Canada and the United States. So big business started to move its operations to other countries where labour costs were cheaper. It was a good business decision and it didn't hurt the senior executives any. In fact, it made for bigger profits overall and larger bonuses to *them*. But suddenly, North American jobs started to fall by the wayside and that's one of the major reasons why we have high unemployment today."

"You're saying," said Logan, "that by moving business to other countries, jobs were lost in North America."

"Exactly," said Uncle Bill. "It's all part of 'globalization' and here's my point: Government in North America touts globalization as a good thing but I'm not so sure they're right."

"What would you rather see, Uncle Bill?" asked Logan.

"I'd rather see a system that encourages people to buy North American-made goods. If everybody bought North American, we'd put our own labour force back to work and there'd be a heck of a lot more out there for young people rather than the McJobs we've been talking about for the last year."

"What exactly is free-trade, and is it bad for us?" asked Logan.

"Free trade occurs when goods manufactured in one country can be sold into the other and vice versa without government tariffs that would increase the cost of these goods to consumers in the second country," replied Uncle Bill.

"I personally don't think free trade between Canada and the U.S. is bad," he continued. "Mine may not be the most popular view, but I believe we need a strong *North American economy* and, if we had that, there would be enough manufacturing in Canada to keep us happy because the Americans would buy from us as we would buy from them."

"What about Mexico?" I asked.

"Ah," said Uncle Bill, "I see you've been reading the papers. From an American's perspective, Mexico is as important, if not more important, than Canada. But unfortunately, from our perspective up here, if the Americans move business activities down into Mexico, or if Canadian companies relocate *their* activities to Mexico because Mexican labour is cheaper, we're going to suffer a heck of a lot. So, I guess if *I* were making policy, from a selfish Canadian standpoint, I really wouldn't want to see a strategic alliance with Mexico. Over the next 10 or 20 years, it could make *our* unemployment worse."

"So, is the loss of jobs to countries where labour costs are cheaper the only reason we've got problems?" asked Logan.

"Unfortunately, Logan, it's not all that simple. There's another major factor."

"What's that?" I asked.

"The inflation we had in the '70s meant that a lot of people around my age got huge raises year after year for several years in a row. It wasn't uncommon for people to have their incomes go up 12 to 15 per cent each year, without any increase in productivity or any change in job description or any promotion. The problem is, after 20 years or so in the work force, by the time many people reached their late 40s or early 50s, they were earning so much money their employers couldn't afford to keep them. This is why so many people my age got laid off over the last 10 years."

HE NEEDS CHEERING UP—
TELL HIM THAT THE SPIRAL
OF INFLATION, GLOBALIZATION
AND THE ECONOMY IS
MOVING TOWARD
ENTREPRENEURSHIP

"How so?" I asked.

"Well, Andrea, let's pretend you're a department head and you have a person working for you who's been around for 20 years and is earning $45,000 a year."

"Okay," asked Logan, "what's your point?"

"Hang on a second. Let's assume you know full well you could replace the $45,000 a year person with someone fresh out of college who's willing to work the *same job* for $21,000 a year. What would you do?"

"I'd like to think that I'd be loyal to my long-term employee," I said.

"A noble sentiment," replied Uncle Bill. "But if you, in turn, were getting pressure from *your* superior and it boiled down to a choice: either trim your budget or lose *your own job,* what would you do?"

"I see your point, Uncle Bill," I said contritely.

"Now, that's why so many companies have encouraged long-term employees to take early retirement in the prime of their careers. And it isn't only the private sector of big business that's guilty. It's happened in our colleges and universities as well. For someone like me, it's really sad to see people who are still in their 40s who have many productive years left, being forced out of their jobs. Some of them still haven't paid for their homes and often they still have dependent children. And the sad truth is, the older you are, the harder it is to retrain."

"So, what's going to happen to *us,* Uncle Bill?" I asked. "Is all this going to turn around?"

"That's a good question," said Uncle Bill. "In general, I don't think the prognosis is all that good. It seems that government is caught-up with the concept of globalization. It sounds glamorous. It allows the Prime Minister to go trotting off to Munich and Tokyo and it enables senior government officials to get involved in exotic trade missions. I'm afraid that government may not see the need for a retrenching and a shift in emphasis towards a North American-based economy until things get a lot worse."

"You mean the situation is going to get worse before it gets better?" asked Logan.

Uncle Bill shrugged. "Even if government doesn't move, there is some possibility that salvation will come from the education system."

"How so?" I asked.

"Through your schools. The schools today are only beginning to wake up to the realities of life. In many parts of the country, there are courses such as your health and lifestyles program. Schools are beginning to recognize they have a responsibility to ensure that their students know more than just how to read, write, and do arithmetic by the time they graduate. Students have to be taught how to live in the real world. *But the whole focus of education has to change even more!*"

"What do you mean?" asked Logan.

"Historically," said Uncle Bill pounding his hand on the table for emphasis, "the focus of education was always to encourage students to go out and get good jobs. *Well, there ain't a lot of good jobs out there. So the focus has to change.*"

"I know," I said, "*the focus has to move toward entrepreneurship.*"

"You hit the nail right on the head, Andrea," said Uncle Bill with a smile. "And it's finally starting to happen. Some schools are encouraging those kids who have an aptitude toward entrepreneurship to pursue it—to look forward to owning their own businesses rather than working for someone else, and to *go into businesses where people need the goods or services they can provide, whether times are good or bad.*"

"Like in my case," I said. "When I become an optometrist, people are going to need their eyes checked and they're going to need glasses or contact lenses whether times are good or bad."

"That's exactly right," Uncle Bill responded. "You may be one of those relatively few people who'll be able to manage for a whole lifetime without changing careers—although, young lady, you're going to have to keep up with changes in technology. The new laser surgery techniques to cure nearsightedness are becoming far more prevalent and you may actually find that your patient-base becomes smaller over time."

"That's possible, Uncle Bill," I said. "But they said the same thing about dentists when fluoride came into use. Our guidance counsellor told us how, for a short time, students were advised not to go into dentistry because there wouldn't be as many teeth to fill. And yet, based on surveys we've looked at in school, dentists have one of the highest incomes of any professional group."

"That's true," said Uncle Bill with a chuckle. "Dentists are smart. They keep a low profile and nobody knows that, on balance, they probably earn as much as, or more than, many doctors, lawyers, and certainly accountants."

"Do we need to take up a collection for you?" Logan asked.

"No," said Uncle Bill. "Fortunately, I'm not most accountants. But back to the educational system. When I suggest the schools have to encourage entrepreneurship, here's what I mean: *historically, it's always been the poorer students, the underachievers, who have been channelled into shop courses such as auto mechanics. Why shouldn't the school system look for good students who are capable and ambitious and also have good manual skills? Why shouldn't these kids be taught auto mechanics with a view towards not only being able to fix cars, but also towards owning auto body and mechanical repair shops?"*

"I see your point, Uncle Bill. Do you think the day might come when less-gifted students get channelled into white-collar jobs?" asked Logan.

"I don't think that's probable," said Uncle Bill with a laugh, "but nothing would surprise me."

"What are some of the career choices to stay away from?" asked Logan curiously.

"Well, now you're pushing me way beyond my level of expertise. I'm certainly not a career counsellor. But I would strongly suggest if someone is looking for either a career opportunity as an employee or as a business owner, that he or she should look at providing goods or services that are needed *whether times are good or bad*. Also, one might be well-off avoiding careers in industries that are extremely cyclical."

"How so?" I asked.

"Well, for example," said Uncle Bill, "let's look at architecture. In boom times, there's a lot of construction that goes on so architects are quite busy, and if they're busy, presumably they make money. In an economic downturn, there's less construction and architects often don't have a lot to do. Now, there are many professions that operate in cyclical economies. Stockbrokers, for example, tend to make a lot of money in some years and not in others. The same goes for realtors. Doctors and dentists tend to have incomes that are relatively consistent from year to year. Accountants who specialize in bankruptcy law tend to do better in a bad economy than in a good one. And you see these ads in the paper in which liquidators advertise the sale of goods previously sold by companies that have just gone bust. Well, receivers and liquidators do a lot better in bad times than in good."

"It strikes me, Uncle Bill," I said, "that if there's something you want to do, like be an architect, you shouldn't necessarily be put off by the fact that you're going to have good years and bad years. *All you need do is make sure you don't spend every penny you make in the good years and you put something aside for rainy days.*"

"I couldn't have said it better myself," said Uncle Bill. "That's why it's so important to get into a savings program, the way you guys have, early. If you make it a practice to set money aside on a regular basis, not only will there be something there when you retire, but you'll also be able to weather the storm if times get rough. It's impossible to predict the future, at least in the long-term, with any degree of accuracy. Who knows whether there'll be some unforeseen development as a result of which you might actually have to give up your career as an optometrist? If you've got some savings though, you'll be able to roll with the punches, go back to school, re-train, or do whatever is necessary to make you a productive person again. And I can see that it's in your nature to be productive. Anyway, I don't think we can solve all the problems of the country and the world at one breakfast. At least you guys have some direction and an idea of where you're going, so I think we'll end this little session. Besides, I've got a date this afternoon. Believe it or not, I've never gone skating on the Rideau Canal and I understand you can cruise along for miles."

"Can we join you, Uncle Bill?" Logan asked excitedly.

I jabbed my brother in the ribs.

"Maybe some other time, Uncle Bill," I said. "I'm actually booked for a couple of word processing lessons this afternoon and I'm sure Logan's got to clean Kiki's cage."

Chapter Nine

May 2001

Logan's Story: Moving Up—Moving Out

Looking back over the years that I spent at Elgin College taking my marketing diploma, I can certainly say the word 'boredom' wasn't part of my vocabulary. I worked darn hard selling kitchen knives during that four-year period—not so much because it was difficult, but because the hours were long and sporadic. It got so I could deliver my spiel in my sleep, but I found if I didn't keep up the enthusiasm in my voice, I just wouldn't make sales. Fortunately, I had a good product and, in retrospect, I can tell you, I learned a very important lesson. *It's a lot easier to sell something you believe in than something you don't.*

Although going to school and working at the same time is a tough combination, I can't say I didn't have fun too. I discovered outdoor free plays, concerts, camping, and, would you believe, gourmet cooking, much to Mom's delight! Fortunately, I took Uncle Bill's advice and stayed at home, paying my parents the modest amount of $200 a month for room and board. At that time, I didn't know how lucky I was to get away with so little.

When I was 19, I bought myself a used car for $7,300. I'm glad I took Dad's advice to have it checked out carefully before signing the deal. I looked at two other cars first that had both been in serious accidents but had been repaired so the extensive damage was well-hidden. Fortunately, the $50 that I spent on hiring my own mechanic stood me in good stead and I was able to avert disaster. They say, 'third time lucky' and my used Ford Escort proved a reliable mode of transportation.

To tell the truth, my social life wasn't all that great, what with school and working. I found I was neither fish nor fowl.

Some of my high school friends had gone on to university full-time and we no longer had a lot in common. Many of the others who couldn't wait to finish their formal educations and get out into the world to earn a living, were working at low-paying, uninteresting jobs and spent too much time (at least for my liking) in the bars after work and in the evenings, trying to make up for their humdrum days.

I dated a bit, although nothing serious, and, to be honest, managed to have a 'close encounter' on more than one occasion. There are some drawbacks, though, to living at home, if you know what I mean. When I was 20, I was able to get away for two weeks to Fort Lauderdale in the winter and it was a real blast. The next year, I decided to do something more exotic and spent a two-week vacation in Barbados. Believe me, there's nothing like palm trees, the ocean, and a soft breeze in the middle of February!

In April, 2001, a couple of important things happened. First, I finally completed my diploma program and, at the same time, I met Lisa. Now, if this were a romance novel, I would probably be describing her in terms of undying love and devotion—my one and only and so on. Actually, as events eventually unfolded, this wasn't the case at all. We parted company about six months later—on a friendly basis, I might add—but, at the time, things were *pretty interesting*.

Lisa worked as a cosmetician at a department store where she earned around $8 or $9 an hour. It wasn't bad work and, with her bubbly personality, she seemed to get along with most of the customers. But on her income, there was no way she could live on her own and when things started to get somewhat steamy, we decided it might be best if I got my own place. Besides, by this time, I could tell that Dad was getting a little antsy for me to leave. As far as Mom was concerned, I probably could have stuck around forever, and that would have been okay, but Dad was starting to make jokes about grown-up children staying with their parents too long. Once or twice, he deftly left the newspaper open to the vacant apartments section and it wasn't too long before I caught on to his not-so-subtle hints. I started to look for an apartment and had almost signed a lease when the fates smiled on me and I ran into Uncle Bill on my way to my health club. He had just returned from his annual winter vacation at his home in Phoenix and, for a fellow who was already on the 'wrong' side of 50, he sure looked good.

Uncle Bill asked me if I wanted to join him for dinner that night after my work-out. He had remarried two years previously and appeared to be ecstatically happy. He told me his wife, Nora, was in Sarnia for a couple of days helping out her kid sister who had just given birth to her first child. I was happy to take him up on his offer and we agreed to meet early that evening at Chianti for Italian.

❧

Uncle Bill and I both arrived at Chianti promptly at 7:00. We were shown to our table and handed menus. Normally, it was my experience that Uncle Bill usually preferred to eat first and talk after. That night, he surprised me by jumping right in to serious conversation.

"So," said Uncle Bill, "I hear from your Mom you've been apartment-hunting. I gather you think it's time to break away from the nest."

There was something about Uncle Bill's tone that wasn't quite right. I would have expected a greater sense of approval.

"Is there something wrong, Uncle Bill?" I asked. "I thought you'd be happy for me."

"I'm happy you're going out on your own, my boy," he said. "Frankly, it's about time. I remember, a few years ago, we had a discussion, you, me, and Andrea, about the merits of staying home versus going away to school. When I suggested you might be better off financially by staying home, I didn't mean indefinitely."

"So, what's the problem?" I asked in wonderment.

Uncle Bill laughed at the puzzled expression on my face.

"It's not the moving out that's the problem. It's the fact that you're looking for an *apartment*."

"I don't think I'd last too long bedding down on streetcorners,

109

Uncle Bill," I said sarcastically. He impaled me with 'the look'.

"I'm sorry, Uncle Bill," I said. "I didn't mean to be sarcastic but I'm afraid I have no idea what you're thinking. What am I doing wrong?"

"You shouldn't be looking for an apartment," Uncle Bill exclaimed. "For you, that's a sign of unimaginative, anti-survival, anti-prosperity thinking."

I was blown away by my uncle's vehemence.

"What do you mean?" I stammered.

"You should be buying a house," he exclaimed.

"A house?" I asked dumbfounded. "But I'm just 22 years old and single."

"So, what better time is there?" Uncle Bill retorted. "Why wait until you're married and have two kids? *Now's* the ideal time for you."

"But guys my age just don't ..."

"And why not?" interrupted Uncle Bill, raising his eyebrows. *"Having a fully-paid house is a major cornerstone of anybody's financial security and the earlier you start, the better off you'll be.* Especially if you find the right place, for now at least."

"The right place?" I asked dumbfounded.

"Yes, what someone like you needs is a house with a basement suite that can be rented out. Instead of you helping to make a *landlord* wealthy, you can *become* the *landlord* and use your *tenant* to establish *your own wealth."*

"You're going too fast for me, Uncle Bill," I said. "Can we take this one step at a time?"

"Sure," Uncle Bill nodded. "I'm sorry to come down so hard on you, but to tell you the truth, I'm a little miffed with your Mom and Dad."

"Why's that?" I asked.

"Because their thinking is too damn traditional. They didn't buy their house until a year or so after you and Andrea were born, so they figure the logical thing for you to do is to move into an apartment. *That's the way it's always been done—but that doesn't mean that's the right way to go today."*

"I'm afraid you're still losing me, Uncle Bill. Can we slow down?"

110

"Sure," said Uncle Bill, waving the waiter away with a signal that he didn't want to be disturbed. "I've got some stuff to show you," he said, reaching under the table and pulling out a small briefcase which I hadn't even noticed when we'd entered the restaurant. He pulled out a stack of papers and tossed the first one at me.

LOGAN'S EARNINGS, SPENDING & SAVINGS RECORD

		1	- 2	= 3	+ 4	+ 5	= 6
YEAR	AGE BEGINNING OF YEAR	GROSS EARNINGS	AMOUNT SPENT INCL.. TAXES	CURRENT YEAR'S SAVINGS IN MUTUALS	SAVINGS BEGINNING OF YEAR	GROWTH (DECLINE)	SAVINGS END OF YEAR
1995	16	$ 2,400	$ 1,100	$ 1,300	$ -	$ 90	$ 1,390
1996	17	3,900	1,500	2,400	1,390	340	4,130
1997	18	8,200	4,800	3,400	4,130	680	8,210
1998	19	14,000	12,000*	2,000	8,210	1,020	11,230
1999	20	17,000	11,000	6,000	11,230	(400)	16,830
2000	21	22,000	11,500	10,500	16,830	3,800	31,130
2001	22	?					

* Bought a used car for $7,300

It was a summary of my earnings, spending, and savings record since I had first started working back in 1995. My mouth dropped open in surprise.

"Where did you get this from?" I asked.

"I've been keeping track," said Uncle Bill smugly, "since the very beginning."

"But how did you get these numbers?"

"Elementary, my dear Watson," he said with a chuckle. "Who's been doing your income tax return every year?" he asked.

I smacked my head with the palm of my hand as comprehension slowly dawned.

"Of course," I said, "you know my gross earnings from my tax return. But how did you get the rest of the numbers?"

"Who's been administering your mutual fund investments?" he asked.

"Right again," I said.

Uncle Bill smiled. "You see, that's why I'm an accountant. I know what you earned, which is column one; and because I handle your investments for you, I also know how much you've put each year into mutuals, which is column three. I get the growth statement on your behalf and that gives me the figures for column five. I've just assumed the amount spent in column two, which includes your income taxes, is the difference between your earnings year-by-year and your savings. Calculating the accumulated savings at the end of each year is obviously a pretty easy thing to do."

"Right," I interjected.

"It's simply the opening balance in column four plus the growth in column five."

"This is very interesting," I said. "I had an idea that my savings were up around $30,000 but it's nice to see it down on paper."

"That's right," said Uncle Bill. "You can see how your savings have been growing since you first started to earn money. On balance, your mutual funds have returned around 14 per cent, even though 1999 was a dismal year."

"The year the market crashed," I said. "Pretty depressing, wasn't it?"

"I guess it was for a lot of people," said Uncle Bill. "But notice the 22 per cent return last year."

"I remember," I interrupted. "Dollar-cost averaging."

"That's right," Uncle Bill nodded happily. "The fact that you put in money on a regular basis, month after month, means that when the market was down, you were able to buy more shares for your regular monthly investment and, in the long-run, you came out way ahead."

"What's my total earnings for the six years?" I asked.

"$67,500," said Uncle Bill promptly, "and you've managed to save over $25,000, all because you've been living at home. The last couple of years, your spending has increased a lot because you've been operating your own car."

"And taking a couple of vacations too."

"Of course," said Uncle Bill. *"You've got to be able to enjoy earning money by spending as well as saving some of it."*

"So, what's the scoop about me buying a house?" I asked.

"Ah ha," said Uncle Bill. "After I spoke to your Mom last night when I got back from Phoenix and she told me you were moving out, I called Sarah McCutchin, who is Nora's best friend. She sells real estate and is one of the top producers at Adanac Trust. I asked her to scout around for a good property in the $100,000 range which, first of all, would be suitable for my nephew to live in and also would have a basement suite that could be rented out to offset some of the costs. She came up with a couple of properties, but this one here is her top recommendation." Uncle Bill pulled out a listing sheet and waved it in front of my face.

"Let's see," I said.

"You're free to look at it," said Uncle Bill, "but it isn't going to tell you

very much. If you like the idea, we can go look at this place tomorrow morning. We can look at some others also. More importantly, let's go over some of the numbers I've taken the liberty to throw together. Even if you don't buy this property, I'm sure you'll learn a thing or two that will help you in making a decision on what to do."

"I should've known," I said with a mock groan.

"Here, take a look at this. It's pretty easy to understand."

113

Projections for the Purchase of Logan's House

Purchase price			$100,800
Closing costs:	Legal, etc.	$ 715	
	Appraisal fees	235	
	CMHC ins. (2.5% x 90,000)	2,250	3,200
Total cost			104,000
Assumed downpayment			14,000
Mortgage financing @ 8%			$ 90,000
Monthly payment–15 year amortization			$ 853
Monthly taxes			82
Heating			100
Electricity			75
Insurance and miscellaneous			80
Subtotal			1,190
Less: Monthly rental income			450
Net occupancy cost			$ 740

"I'll run through this with you line by line," said Uncle Bill. "The asking price is $103,800, but Sarah said they would probably accept an offer of about $3,000 less. So let's assume a purchase price of $100,800. To that we have to add closing costs."

"What's?..."

Uncle Bill raised his hand to stop me. "That's the legal fees, mortgage documentation, mortgage insurance costs, and so on."

"Mortgage?..."

"Logan," Uncle Bill said patiently, "let me finish, and if you have any questions I'll be happy to answer them after."

I nodded in agreement.

"First, there are the legal fees which will cover the transfer of title, mortgage documentation and so on. Then there is a CMHC appraisal fee of $235. CMHC stands for 'Canada Mortgage and Housing Corporation'. Their job is to insure mortgages so lenders are protected if borrowers default on their obligations. CMHC charges a fee between one-and-a-quarter and two-and-half per cent of the mortgage if the borrower's downpayment is less than 25% of the total price. In your case, it's $2,250. By the way, the appraisal fee covers a valuation report on the property to make sure it's worth at least the amount of the loan. Both CMHC costs on my schedule only have to paid once, which means you won't have to pay them again even when you renew your mortgage down the road. I'll explain 'mortgages' soon, but do you follow me so far?"

I nodded again.

"Okay," he said. "So, we'll assume a total cost of $104,000 and that you make a downpayment of $14,000."

"Where ..."

"From your mutuals. You're going to have to cash in about $20,000 or so in order to make this work."

"But I'll be broke," I wailed.

"No, you won't," said Uncle Bill. "You'll just be *diversifying your investments*. Instead of having all your net worth as $31,000 in mutual funds, in my scenario, you'd have $14,000 invested as equity in your own home."

"But you said I'd have to cash in $20,000."

"Sure," said Uncle Bill. "We should allow about $6,000 to $7,000 for furniture and, believe me, that's for pretty basic stuff. I did some checking and the good news is this particular house comes with a fridge and stove and a washer-dryer."

"Hmm," I said, "that's a good deal. Mom and Dad have already told me I can take my bed, desk and chair and, of course, I've got my own TV and stereo system. They also said they would give me $3,000 as a gift towards buying some furniture."

"Hey, that's really nice," said Uncle Bill with smile. "Even so, you should figure on spending $6,000 or $7,000 of your own money. You're going to want something nice for your living room and you'll also need a kitchen set and a microwave; and you'll be amazed at how much it costs just to equip yourself with kitchen utensils, even if your knives are free."

"But there goes my savings," I moaned, immediately becoming quite depressed.

"Now, don't get upset," said Uncle Bill. "You'll still have over $10,000 in mutual funds when this is done and $14,000 equity in your house."

"But that's only $24,000."

"True, the other $6,000 or $7,000 will go towards furniture and your furniture will, in fact, depreciate. When I got you and your sister into saving programs a few years ago, I never tried to imply that these savings are forever. Sure, your objective is to have plenty of money for long-term goals and ultimately you want to guarantee a comfortable retirement. But that's way down the road and it's pretty hard at your age to think in those terms. Just think about it. Everybody has to buy furniture at some point in time *and if you didn't have your mutual funds now, what would you have to do—even if you rented an apartment,* which is what you were going to do in the first place?"

"I suppose I'd need the same furniture," I said slowly, "and I guess I'd have to do what all my friends and acquaintances have done and that's *borrow the money.* Hey," I blurted out as comprehension finally hit, *"I don't have to go into hock to buy furniture; I'm way ahead of my friends!"*

"You got it," said Uncle Bill beaming. "Now, I'd like to tell you something I think I should at least mention, although I don't really recommend it in your case."

"What's that?"

"It might surprise you to know," said Uncle Bill, "that you don't actually have to sell any of your mutual funds to buy your house."

"How so?" I asked.

"You can use leverage if you want to."

"Leverage?"

"That's right. By putting up your mutual funds as *collateral,* you could *borrow* $20,000 and use that money towards your downpayment and your furniture costs."

"But if I borrow, won't I have to pay interest?"

"You would," said Uncle Bill, "but at what rate?"

"I'm not sure," I answered. "You tell me."

"I checked with my bank," said Uncle Bill. "Today, with $30,000 of collateral, you could borrow $20,000 and pay about eight per cent."

"Why would I want to do that, though?"

"In theory," replied Uncle Bill, "if your mutual funds grow at 12 per cent ..."

"I'd be ahead by four per cent," I completed his sentence.

"That's right. But what's the drawback?" he asked.

I thought for a moment and the light bulb again went on. "What if the mutual funds drop in value?"

"Exactly," said Uncle Bill. "If you use leverage, there's a risk factor. Also," he continued, "you'd have to pay the interest out of your ongoing income and I think this would hurt your cash flow."

"Cash flow?" I asked.

"Yes, your cash flow is your after-tax income and how you spend it. I suspect things may be a bit tight for you, at least in the first couple of years. But you'll find, if you let me complete my analysis, it's going to be well worth your while to buy the house *now.* The most conservative thing for you to do is to use part of your mutual fund investments towards the house and furniture. You'll still have $10,000 left."

"It doesn't seem like that much."

"Really? How old are you?"

"Just turned 22. Why?"

"Remember all those years ago when I showed you the table on the compound amount of $1?"

"Sure I remember," I said.

"I checked in that book by Zimmer that I still have, 'The Money Manager for Canadians', and if you continue to average 12 per cent on your $10,000 mutual funds investment, in 40 years at your age 62, *even if you don't add one penny to your savings for the rest of your life, you'd still have $930,000 at the end."*

"Wow," I said, "I suppose since you put it that way, I shouldn't be too upset."

"That's right," said Uncle Bill. "How many other 22-year-olds do you know who have $10,000 in mutual funds and $20,000 invested in a house and furniture?"

"I guess I haven't done too badly so far, thanks to you," I added. I could see my uncle blush slightly, even in the soft light of the restaurant.

"Okay," I said, as I grew more enthusiastic. "Let's assume I buy this house for $104,000 including closing costs and make a downpayment of $14,000, and buy my furniture. Let's go through the rest of your numbers. I think I can handle it now."

"Good," said Uncle Bill turning his attention to his projections sheet. "If you put down $14,000, you'd be left with a mortgage of $90,000."

"What exactly is a mortgage?" I asked. "I know we discussed them a long time ago but I've forgotten. It really wasn't all that important at the time."

"A mortgage is simply a loan," said Uncle Bill, "that a lending institution makes to enable a buyer to buy real estate, where the real estate itself is the collateral."

"*Collateral?*" I asked.

"Yes, the *security*. In other words, if the borrower defaults on his or her payments, the lender can take the property away in settlement of the debt. So, if you didn't make your payments, you'd lose your house and your equity investment would go up in smoke."

"I can tell you that's not going to happen!" I exclaimed.

"Certainly not," said Uncle Bill bending his head down towards the paper. "Now, you should be able to get a five year locked-in mortgage at a rate of eight per cent."

"Five years? Locked-in? What do you mean?"

"Well," said Uncle Bill, "there are all kinds of possibilities. You can get a mortgage that has a six-month term only. That means it's renewed at whatever the prevailing rate is six months down the line; or you can get a one-year term, a two-year term, three years, four years, and some institutions even give as many as seven years."

"Why do you recommend a five-year term?" I asked.

"The rate for a five-year term is only about one-and-a-half per cent, or 'points' as they're called, higher than the rate for a six-month term and the trouble is, interest rates can fluctuate quite quickly and quite widely. In my opinion, many people make the mistake of going with the lower rate and run the risk of getting caught if interest rates suddenly start to skyrocket. In my view, *the spread of one-and-a-half per cent between the short-term rate and the long-term rate isn't an interest cost; it's an insurance policy...*"

"So if rates go up," I said, "I'm protected."

"That's right," said Uncle Bill. "Today, our economy is really very uncertain. It's been that way for years now. I believe peace of mind is worth a heck of a lot and knowing exactly where you stand for a five-year period is a lot more comfortable than having to panic every Tuesday when the Bank of Canada sets the interest rate for the next week."

"So," I said, "I should try to pay off my $90,000 mortgage over five years."

Uncle Bill laughed. "I wish it were that easy," he said. "Unfortunately, unless you start to make a great deal of money very quickly, it's not realistic for you to pay off your house over five years. In fact, I've targeted for a 15-year payout."

"I'm confused," I said. "First you talk five years; now you're talking 15."

"I'll explain," said Uncle Bill. "What I suggest is that you lock into a *fixed-rate* for a five-year period. This means for the next five years, you'd know exactly what your monthly payment is. After five years, your mortgage would be renewed at the prevailing interest rate. If you're lucky, rates will stay down. If you're unlucky, rates will be higher."

My face dropped at that last statement.

"But if rates are higher," said Uncle Bill, "in all probability, this would mean we're having a bout of inflation. And if interest rates go up in inflationary times, so do wages. In any event, you can cross that bridge when you get to it. I'll tell you more about inflation and interest rates a little bit later. Anyway," he continued, "you should lock into a rate for five years, but you should *also* target to have your mortgage paid off, for now at least, over 15 years. If you start to make a lot of money, you may want to pay your house off that much more quickly, although, come to think of it, in all probability, this first house won't be your last one."

"So, what's the point?" I asked.

"The point is, by establishing equity in this house, you'll be able to sell it eventually and use that equity to trade-up to a nicer house."

"I see where you're coming from," I said. "I just thought of something though," I continued.

"What's that?"

"I overheard Mom and Dad talking once, about paying off their house over 25 years. In fact, they still have a few years left to go before their house is fully paid."

Uncle Bill shook his head in disgust. "That's where people get screwed up by following conventional wisdom."

"Why's that?"

"It's true," said Uncle Bill, "that if you arrange a 25 year payout, which is also referred to as a 25-year *'amortization'* of your mortgage, your monthly payments will in fact be cheaper. *But you get killed by the amount of interest you have to pay because you're paying for a much longer time.*"

Uncle Bill chuckled and pulled out another piece of paper. "Let's leave this first analysis on the projections of your house purchase for a moment and take a look at the alternatives of paying off a house over 15 years versus 25 years."

"You sly devil, you. You anticipated this discussion all along." Uncle Bill simply smiled and shrugged.

COMPARISON OF LOGAN'S TOTAL MORTGAGE PAYMENTS WITH 25- AND 15-YEAR AMORTIZATIONS

$90,000 AT 8 %	15-YEAR AMORTIZATION	25-YEAR AMORTIZATION
Monthly payment	$ 853	$ 686
Annual cost (monthly x 12)	10,236	8,232
Total cost		
($ 8,232 x 25)		205,800
($10,236 x 15)	153,540	
Total interest paid		
(Total cost less $90,000 principal)	$ 63,540	$115,800
Monthly payment:	$ 853 minus $686 =	$ 167
Total interest:	$115,800 minus $63,540 =	$ 52,260

"Now," he said. "Assuming you finance $90,000 at eight per cent, if you go for a 25-year amortization your monthly payments are $686 against $853 over 15 years."

"Where am I going to get that kind of money from each month?"

"We'll go back to the other analysis in just a minute or two," said Uncle Bill soothingly. "Remember, we have to factor in the assumption that you'll be renting out your basement. Also, consider that part of your payments goes toward paying interest, which I suppose you might see as lost money, *but the rest of it goes towards paying off the debt itself. Over time, you build up equity—* in other words, your own wealth."

"I see," I said. "I won't panic just yet. Please carry on."

"Okay," said Uncle Bill, "you've got your monthly payments under both alternatives. Then, what I've done, is I've calculated the annual cost. It's simply the monthly payment multiplied by 12. The next calculation is the total cost. In the case of the 25-year term, it's $8,232 times 25 years. In the case of the 15-year term, it's $10,236 times only 15 years."

"Wow," I said jumping ahead, "there's quite a difference in the total interest paid."

"That's right," replied Uncle Bill. *"For the sake of $167 more a month, by paying off over 15 years instead of 25 years you'd save over $50,000."*

"That's unbelievable," I said.

"It's true, though. *It's really nothing more than the power* of *compound interest that I taught you and Andrea so many years ago, working in reverse.* In this case, the power of compound interest benefits the lending institution when people are foolish enough to extend their mortgages longer than they have to. I tried to tell your Mom and Dad a couple of times they'd be better off paying *their* mortgage much more quickly but, to be truthful, I didn't get anywhere and I really didn't want to push."

"Maybe you can't teach old dogs new tricks," I said.

"Sometimes yes, sometimes no," said Uncle Bill. "Although I suppose it's easier to start learning when you're just a puppy like yourself."

"Okay," I said, "you've convinced me. I'd certainly be in better shape paying off my house quickly rather than slowly."

"Good," said Uncle Bill. "You can pay off your mortgage even quicker by paying twice a month instead of monthly, or by using other acceleration programs that various lending institutions have in place, but for now, let's assume a monthly payment of $853." He turned back to his projection sheet. "We also have to take into account taxes, heating, electricity and insurance. I've taken the liberty of getting the numbers from Sarah and converting them from annual to monthly costs. You can see you're looking at just under $1,200 a month, all inclusive. But if we subtract the monthly rent for the basement suite, your *net occupancy cost* is less than $750."

"Wow," I said, "that's still a heck of a lot of money."

"True, but you should be able to afford it. If you were ever afraid of running short, you could also look at having a roommate for a while. That's one of the benefits of owning your own home. If you have an apartment, there are usually restrictions against subletting. A roommate can help with the yard work and help pay a percentage of the utilities. By the way, what do you expect to be earning now that you've graduated?"

"Well, I never got a chance to tell you my good news," I said. "The company I've been working for has appointed me branch manager. The previous guy is moving to Halifax to open an office there. I won't have to go out selling any more but I'll still be getting a commission based on the performance of my staff. Here I am, 22 years old, and I'll have seven people working for me!"

"So, how well do you think you'll do financially?" Uncle Bill asked me.

"Minimum $40,000 the first year, I expect. I've got it made in the shade, don't I?"

"For now you do," said Uncle Bill, "but let's take things one step at a time. I have a suspicion, after a couple of years, $40,000, or even $50,000 or $60,000, won't be enough for you. You'll realize you've got much greater potential than that."

"Maybe so, Uncle Bill, but for now you're looking at one happy camper. The only thing is, I remember way back when, you showed me how foolish I was to assume I could have a house, a family and a Porsche on $70,000 a year...."

"Not foolish," interrupted Uncle Bill, "just uninformed."

"So, how can you be sure I can afford a house, and even my second-hand car, on an income of $40,000 a year?"

"I have an idea you'll be able to make it," said Uncle Bill, "but we won't know for sure until we do a budget. I'll tell you, though, for the next few years, your investment focus is going to have to change."

"What do you mean?" I asked.

"Well, up to now," replied Uncle Bill, "you've been buying mutual funds with your savings. For the next few years, you'll be plowing most of your excess earnings into your house. Here let me show you." He again pulled out another piece of paper.

"You've been working hard while I've been at the gym," I said.

"You know us old accountants. We love to play with numbers."

"I just realized something funny, Uncle Bill. When I took math at school, most of the time I found the stuff boring. *But it isn't boring when you see your own figures in front of you.*"

"You've hit the nail on the head, my boy," Uncle Bill replied. "*If people can just do away with their innate suspicion of numbers and confront their own financial situations the way **you're** doing, they'd be a lot better off. And you know the irony is you don't need higher mathematics. The only thing you need is the ability to add, subtract, multiply, and divide, and, for that, a simple hand-held calculator will suffice.*"

"You're right. It isn't complicated. And to tell the truth, it's fun. Why do you think they always glamorize lawyers on TV and never accountants?"

"More reactionary thinking," said Uncle Bill. "I guess accountants are really just the unsung heroes of our society."

"Okay," I said, "we'll look at this next set of numbers. But if it's okay with you, I'd like to take a break and have supper first. I'm starving."

"Yes, I know," said Uncle Bill, "you're a growing boy and all that."

"I've found, since I've joined the health club, I've been eating more but I haven't gained any weight. My girlfriend sure likes my physique," I said as I pumped up a muscle. "You know," I continued, "here I am just a couple of years out of high school and, from time to time, I run into some of my former classmates. Would you believe some of the guys are already starting to develop beer bellies, and a couple of the girls, especially the ones who've had kids, sure don't look the same as they did a few years ago."

"It's sad," Uncle Bill sighed, "how a lot of people just let themselves go. In school, I suppose phys-ed is a compulsory course. But so many people just don't keep up the good work after they leave. There isn't a whole lot of benefit in making money if you're not going to take care of yourself."

"You're right. I feel sorry for the poor suckers who throw away their money chain smoking in the bars."

"Fortunately, a lot of young people *do* take care of themselves and, if *you* stay with it, you'll look like your Uncle Bill someday." He laughed as I cringed.

"Actually, Uncle Bill, for a guy who's almost as old as Mick Jagger, you're not doing too badly."

❧

Uncle Bill signalled the waiter and we ordered caesar salad appetizers and pasta as the main course. The food came quickly and we hunkered down for some serious eating. I tried to relax and take my mind off our heavy discussion but my thoughts kept returning to the mystery of 'The Budget'. I was afraid that, after building my hopes up, I'd find I couldn't really afford to become a home owner.

"Okay," said Uncle Bill, pushing his empty plate away. "Let's just go through this one last set of numbers and then we'll have dessert."

He shoved a piece of paper over so I could read it.

LOGAN'S NET OCCUPANCY COST PER MONTH OVER FIVE YEARS

Net occupancy cost per month		$ 740
		x12
Net occupancy cost per year		$ 8,880
Net occupancy cost over five years		$44,400
Mortgage outstanding at end of fifth year		
$90,000 x .786	$70,740	
Mortgage pay-down over five years:	$90,000 – $70,740	$19,260
"Real" net occupancy cost		$25,140
Average cost per month over five years:	$25,140 ÷ 60 months	$ 419

"Now," he continued. "At the top of this page, we have your net occupancy cost per month multiplied by 12. That comes to just under $9,000 a year. Over the next five years, you'll spend about $45,000....."

"On housing alone! That's more than I've spent in the last six years on everything together!" I started to go into shock.

"Hold on a second, Logan," Uncle Bill said. "Look at the rest of this. At the end of the fifth year, your mortgage balance will be just under $71,000. In other words, you will have paid down over $19,000 in principal by assuming these monthly costs of $740. The factor of .786 comes from a mortgage table book that tells you how much is owing at the end of each year. It's useful if you want to calculate your equity buildup."

"You mean, even if the house doesn't appreciate in value, my equity, instead of being $14,000, will be a whopping $33,000 after five years?"

"That's right," said Uncle Bill. "So, your real net occupancy cost over five years is only $25,000. That works out to just over $400 a month."

"I don't believe it," I said. "You mean over five years, *my final cost would be less than if I went out today to rent an apartment?*"

"Right again," said Uncle Bill. "This is the real benefit of home ownership. And to top it off," he continued, "what do you think would happen if your house appreciated by say, four and a half per cent a year, on average?"

"Four and a half per cent times five years, that's what? 22 per cent in total... ignoring the effect of compounding. You mean *with* compounding, my $100,000 house would then be worth around $125,000?"

"And if you made a $25,000 profit, what would your *net* cost of living there be?"

"Zero," I said dumbfounded. "Between $25,000 of appreciation and $19,000 of mortgage principal payments, I'd recover the entire $44,000 it cost me to live there over five years! Uncle Bill, you're a genius."

"That may be true, young fellow." He chuckled. "But remember the appreciation isn't guaranteed. I'd be pretty shocked, though, if you didn't come out substantially ahead."

DEAR DIARY — TODAY
I MOVED INTO MY
FIRST HOUSE — WONDERFUL
FEELING — NO MORE WORRIES

Wicks

"You've convinced me, Uncle Bill. Do you have some time tomorrow morning and we'll go look at that house?"

"I've already made an appointment for 10:00. You can pick me up at a quarter to, and we should get there on time. We'll also get a chance to look at two or three other houses so you can

126

see what you like and do some comparisons."

Uncle Bill signalled for the waiter to order dessert. I couldn't help but wonder whether I was being manipulated...just slightly...but I quickly realized it was all for my own good.

CHAPTER TEN

LOGAN'S STORY: LATER THAT EVENING— BUILDING A BUDGET

THERE WAS ONE MORE ITEM Uncle Bill had to introduce me to that wonderful evening he convinced me to become a property owner. It was the idea of building a budget. I recall I was a bit apprehensive at the time. My head was already swimming in numbers, but I guess I had enough sense to realize I wouldn't feel comfortable buying a house unless I really felt that I could swing it. I had never worried too much about my spending because, for a mere $200 a month, Mom and Dad gave me room and board. I did buy my own clothes, although once in a while—maybe even more than once in a while—Mom would surprise me with a few new shirts, a couple of pairs of pants and, if the truth be told, a suit or sports jacket or two. I did pay my own car expenses, but, like I say, I never really worried too much about money.

What I learned though, very quickly, (and this is why that evening stands out so much in my mind) was the *importance of understanding my own set of numbers.* Over the years, Uncle Bill and I (and Andrea too) talked about this concept. We all realize there are many people who are hard-working, reasonably intelligent, but perhaps not highly aware, who are hopelessly beating themselves up, and sometimes everyone around them, because *they* didn't reach some undefined measure of financial and personal success and felt like failures. In a way, it seems that a lot of people beat themselves up because they concentrate on a *career goal,* not a *financial goal.* All it would have taken is learning how to save and the discipline to follow through on effective financial planning. Instead of burying their heads in the sand, if people would just prepare budgets, they'd have a pretty good idea of where they stand. They could then compare their incomes to their projected expenditures and set savings goals. If their expenses are too high, they'd have two choices: either they could earn more money by moonlighting, changing jobs, going into their own businesses or what have you; or they could cut back on spending.

But you can't do all this without a plan. Uncle Bill wasn't kidding when he said the accountants are the unsung heroes of our society. Accountants have evolved the proper tools and it's up to the rest of us to learn to use them. Fortunately, today, the schools are taking a larger role in the development of personal financial planning programs. The education system has finally come to realize one shouldn't wait until age 40 or 50 before paying attention to this process.

Thank goodness for Uncle Bill, because Andrea and I were way ahead of most of our peers.

❧

I finished off dinner with a slice of cheesecake while Uncle Bill had creme caramel and coffee. Uncle Bill put down his fork, swallowed a burp, and then languidly reached back into his briefcase, pulling out a little book.

"Remember this fellow Zimmer, the guy who wrote that math book I showed you when we talked about the power of compound interest?"

I nodded.

"Well, he also put together this book a number of years ago," Bill said, peering at the cover through his reading glasses. "It's called *'Your Canadian Guide to Planning for Financial Security'*."

He held it up and showed me the cover.

"This book contains a number of worksheets people can use, even if they don't have a fancy computer, to make various calculations. I've used it myself over the years for some of the applications. Take a look." He flipped through the book. "Here's a schedule he set up that shows you how to do a personal budget. Zimmer started with the seven categories for spending that the government uses to calculate the consumer price index...Ah, here it is on page 53. The consumer price index tells us how the average Canadian family spends its money and Statistics Canada uses it to measure how prices in each category change from month to month."

The Consumer Price Index
HOW THE AVERAGE CANADIAN FAMILY ALLOCATES ITS DISPOSABLE INCOME
(BASED ON 1986 SPENDING PATTERNS)

CATEGORY	PERCENTAGE
Housing	36.3
Food	18.1
Transportation	18.3
Clothing	8.7
Recreation, reading & education	8.8
Tobacco & alcohol	5.6
Health & personal care	4.2
TOTAL	100.0

"For the budget itself, Zimmer expanded the categories to include their components," Uncle Bill continued. "For example, he broke down housing to include mortgage payments, property taxes, heating and so on. He distinguished between food eaten at home and food consumed away under food costs. Here's a blank schedule on page 50 we can use for your budgeting. Zimmer added an extra category he called 'other' that covers gifts to friends and family, insurance premiums and so on—whatever doesn't fit naturally into any other category. In your case, since you don't have any dependents, you really don't need life insurance, although we should budget for things like birthday gifts and Christmas presents."

I saved that blank form the same way I've saved every document Uncle Bill and I have prepared over the years. Andrea has done the same. We've included it here so you can see the model and use it if you like. I also figure you might be able to understand my initial fear and shock when I saw the form. I mean my reaction was 'gasp—do I have to detail all this stuff?' In retrospect, all I can say is: easier *done* than *said*.

SCHEDULE OF PERSONAL EXPENSES

HOUSING

Rent/Mortgage payments $ _____

  Mortgage principal $ _____

  Mortgage interest   _____

Property taxes   _____

Heating   _____

Electricity   _____

Insurance   _____

Maintenance and improvements   _____

Furnishings and appliances   _____

Telephone   _____

Water   _____

TV rental or cable   _____

Other   _____ $ _____

FOOD

At home   _____

Away   _____   _____

TRANSPORTATION

Public transportation   _____

Automobile

  Car payments/rentals   _____

  Gas and oil   _____

  Insurance   _____

  Licence   _____

  Repairs and maintenance   _____

  Tires   _____   _____

CLOTHING

Purchases   _____

Laundry and cleaning   _____   _____

RECREATION, READING AND EDUCATION

Travel and vacation   _____

Club memberships and dues   _____

Miscellaneous   _____

Babysitting (non-deductible)   _____

Education   _____

  Tuition fees (for children not eligible for tax credits)   _____

  Books   _____

  Miscellaneous   _____

Reading material   _____   _____

TOBACCO AND ALCOHOL

Tobacco   _____

Alcohol   _____   _____

HEALTH AND PERSONAL CARE

Medicine & medical services not covered

  by insurance   _____

Medical and dental insurance premiums   _____

Dental care not covered by insurance   _____

Grooming   _____   _____

OTHER

Gifts to friends and family   _____

Insurance premiums

  Life (Annual increase
  in CSV $ _____)   _____

  Disability   _____

  Liability   _____

Other: _____   _____   _____

TOTAL PERSONAL EXPENDITURES $ _____

"Whoa. That's pretty intimidating, Uncle Bill."

"Piece of cake, son. Even if it isn't penny-perfect, your budget will give you a good idea of where you stand and you'll be able to see whether or not you can really afford to buy a house. Besides, with a little concentration, you can estimate fairly accurately what you spend on different things during the course of the year even if you don't have a whole lot of history to rely on."

"But thinking ahead a year at a time feels so strange," I said. "I've been living in a sheltered cocoon for quite a while—my whole life in fact. And, so far, it's been pretty easy. I earn money, give my parents the $200 a month they've asked for, and then I've got lots left over to cover my car expenses, entertainment and a nice vacation. I'm not sure I'm going to enjoy the responsibility of home ownership."

"Don't set your sights too short-term, son, because, if you do, you won't plan effectively for your future. A little bit of effort is going to pay off for you because you'll get a much better idea where you stand. Besides, if we work through it together, you'll see it won't take you more than 10 or 15 minutes. Like I said before, it doesn't have to be penny-perfect."

"Do we do this monthly?" I asked.

"No," Uncle Bill responded with a chuckle. "We don't have to make you into any more of an accountant, or financial planner for that matter, than is absolutely necessary. It's certainly okay to make your calculations on an annual basis because, earlier tonight, when you told me what your projected income was, you didn't say you're gonna earn $3,300 a month; you said $40,000 a year. So why don't we do everything on an annual basis? Bear with me, it won't take too long. We can use this blank form and we'll just slot in the numbers in pencil."

Uncle Bill reached into his pocket and pulled out a beautiful rosewood mechanical pencil.

"Okay, let's start," he said. "Under housing, we have your mortgage payments which are $853 times 12, which is $10,236. But we have to subtract your rental income which is going to be $450 times 12, or $5,400. So under your rent/mortgage payments we'll put down the difference of $4,836."

"I see," I said. "It's $853 minus $450, times 12."

"Exactly," said Uncle Bill nodding his head. "Now, property taxes are $984 a year and annual heating works out at about $1,200; $75 a month or $900 a year will cover your electricity."

The numbers started to fill up the sheet.

"I told you I got these figures from Sarah when I spoke to her this afternoon. For insurance and miscellaneous, we'll figure $80 a month, $960 a year. That should cover cable TV and so on. You won't have to budget for furniture costs because you'll be buying your furniture up front, and I think you can probably do most of your maintenance and repairs pretty inexpensively. If you need to paint, a little 'sweat equity' never hurt. Now, what about food? You see the two categories here?"

"I don't know," I said, "you tell me."

"Well, I think a single person, even if he or she entertains every now and then, should be able to get by on about $100 a week, broken down as, say, $60 a week for food at home and $40 a week for eating out. Now, obviously, if you're on a really tight budget you can certainly cut back on the eating out part."

"Okay," I said, "a total of $100 a week—that's $5,200 a year."

"Right," said Uncle Bill. "Let's move onto transportation."

"Public transportation. I don't use that. I've got my own car," I said proudly.

"All right, what are your car expenses?"

"I don't have any car payments," I said.

"But we do have to factor in car payments."

"I don't understand," I interrupted.

"Well, your car isn't going to last forever and I think this is one of the very important points you should learn from the idea of preparing a budget. *A budget doesn't only cover what you're spending today; it has to deal with what you're going to spend in the foreseeable future.* For example, you have to take into account the fact that in six months' time, in the winter, you may want to take a holiday. You naturally set aside money for this, don't you?" Uncle Bill didn't wait for my reply. He was in full lecture mode. "So, even if you aren't making car payments today, you should still budget to set aside money each and every month. Then, when you do have to replace your car, the money is there. If you can avoid financing an automobile, you're going to be well ahead of the game."

"What do you think I should put down?"

"I think you should allot $200 a month, which is $2,400 a year."

"And what do I do with that?"

"You should be able to answer your own question," said Uncle Bill.

"Of course," I said, "mutual funds. If I set up *a separate savings plan* where I force myself to put aside $200 a month, when the time comes in two or three years to buy a new car, I'll have that money plus my trade-in. Uncle Bill, you're a genius."

"It's just common sense, Logan."

"Okay, then $200 a month, $2,400 a year, it is. Now, my gas and oil should run about $100 a month. One of the good things about working in an office is that I won't have to do as much travel as I did before, going from house to house selling these knives. It'll be nice to have people come to *me* for a change."

"I suspect that'll be okay for a while," said Uncle Bill, "although, if I know you, I don't think you're going to want to spend all your time sitting in one place. But that's another story. So, let's budget $1,200 a year for gas and oil. Car insurance. What does that set you back?"

"Well, since I'm still under 25, it's pretty expensive. I pay $1,600 a year. I have full coverage in case I hurt somebody else or do any damage but I've insured my own car with a $1,000 deductible."

"That's pretty smart," said Uncle Bill, "especially since your car is already six or seven years old. One of the few good things about getting older is you'll find your car insurance drops. Let's add $75 for your annual licence and $750 for repairs and maintenance."

"That should cover it, tires included."

"Right," said Uncle Bill. "We'll move on to clothing."

"Well, fortunately, I don't need a whole lot of stuff," I said. "I figure $1,500 a year should do it."

"You're now a junior executive, which means you probably should be prepared to buy at least one, if not two, new suits during the course of the year."

"Uggh," I said.

"Well, at least a couple of sports jackets and nice slacks," replied Uncle Bill. "Let's put down $2,000 for clothing purchases and let's allow $30 a month for laundry and dry cleaning."

"I suppose you're right. I can't expect Mom to iron my shirts any more, now that I'm moving out on my own."

"It probably won't hurt you to do some ironing yourself," said Uncle Bill. "If you give everything to the laundry, it's going to cost you way more."

"Okay, we've got that out of the way," I said. "What's the next category?"

"Recreation, reading, and education," Uncle Bill said.

"Travel and vacations...Uhm...Last year, it cost me about $2,400 for two wonderful weeks in Barbados. This year, I'd like to go to Aruba and I think the cost will be about the same."

Uncle Bill nodded as he wrote in the numbers.

"Now, club memberships. The health club runs about $900 a year and then for miscellaneous entertainment, I suppose it's fair for me to allow myself $100 a month."

"That's over and above eating out?" asked Uncle Bill.

"Well, let's still put down $1,200 for the year and we'll see how this fits."

"Good," Uncle Bill nodded approvingly. "You're starting to understand how a budget really works. Sometimes you have expenses that are unavoidable. We accountants call them 'non-discretionary'. In other words, your rent, or if you own a home, your mortgage payment. But in some cases, you have flexibility. And recognizing where you can either cut back or add on is extremely important. If you can't afford $100 a month plus $40 a week for eating out, this is the first area where you can cut back."

"Instead of cutting back, I could always get a roomie for a while, as you suggested," I said.

"True," replied Uncle Bill. "I once knew a woman who bought a three-bedroom house while still in college. She rented both spare bedrooms to friends and managed to live almost free. Not only that, she was able to pay off her house in record time. She owns quite a few rental properties today and doesn't even have to work to support herself....Hmm....Maybe I should look her up...it's been quite a while....Anyway, it's getting late so let's get back to your budget."

"Fortunately," I said, moving down the list, "I don't have any babysitting expenses nor do I have to pay for education any more. Reading material... well, that's probably negligible, a magazine or newspaper here and there. I get most of my books out of the library."

"Okay, then, what about tobacco and alcohol?"

"I'm happy to say my costs here, for all intents and purposes, are zero. I guess I've included the cost of the odd beer or wine cooler in the $100 a month for miscellaneous entertainment."

"That's good," said Uncle Bill. "Take a look at the consumer price index numbers on this piece of paper that I showed you a few minutes ago. *The average Canadian family spends more than five and a half per cent of its income on tobacco and alcohol. Now, if you consider that some people, like yourself, don't smoke and drink, others must be spending upwards of 10 per cent! And that can be the difference between a very comfortable retirement down the line and a hand-to-mouth existence."*

"I suppose you're right, Uncle Bill, but then again," I said with a bit of a laugh, "if you smoke and drink heavily, you don't have to worry as much about retirement."

"How so?" said Uncle Bill, falling into my trap.

"You won't live as long," I answered.

"Arrg," said Uncle Bill, in a cross between a laugh and a groan. "Let's move on....Health and personal care. First, we have medicine and medical services not covered by insurance."

"I'm pretty healthy, I suppose," I said, "but I guess I've got to buy Tylenol, the odd prescription if I get a cold in the winter and so on. Let's put down $200 a year."

"Medical and dental insurance premiums?"

"We have a Blue Cross plan at work that costs $25 a month for a single person and, now that I'm out on my own, I think I'll sign up for it."

"Good, that's $300. We'll also allow $400 for provincial health care costs.... Dental care not covered by insurance?"

"Well, thank goodness for fluoridated water and the fact that I've learned to brush and floss."

"Gee, you're good," cooed Uncle Bill.

"I guess Mom's harping paid off after all. I don't think I'll have to pay more than, oh, a few hundred bucks a year towards my dentist's retirement program."

"Okay, we'll put down another $400 along with $200 for haircuts and so on. What's left?"

"This last category called 'other'," I answered. "The insurance stuff doesn't really apply to me..."

"Not until later on, if and when you have dependents," said Uncle Bill, "but you should budget for gifts to friends and family."

"Right, let's assume about $500 a year. That should cover it."

"Okay, we'll add it all up. You'll notice it only took us about

10 or 15 minutes. At the risk of being overly repetitious, let me again remind you a budget doesn't have to be completely accurate as long as the person or people preparing it have put some thought into it. It's a good starting point. Here, I'll do the honours."

Uncle Bill took my schedule, pulled a little calculator from his briefcase and quickly punched in all the numbers. "Would you care to guess at the total?" he asked after a couple of minutes.

"I sure hope it's under $30,000."

"Why that figure?"

"Well, on my projected earnings of $40,000 a year, I guess my deductions for income tax, Canada Pension and Unemployment Insurance and all that stuff will run about $10,000. That leaves me $30,000 a year for spending and saving."

"Then you should be in reasonably good shape," said Uncle Bill as he showed me the total. "It comes to just under $29,000."

LOGAN'S BUDGET

HOUSING			
Mortgage payments	$853 x 12	$10,236	
Less: rental income	$450 x 12	(5,400)	
		4,836	
Property taxes	$ 82 x 12	984	
Heating	$100 x 12	1,200	
Electricity	$ 75 x 12	900	
Insurance & misc.	$ 80 x 12	960	$8,880
FOOD			
At home	$ 60 x 52	3,120	
Away	$ 40 x 52	2,080	5,200
TRANSPORTATION			
Car payments	$200 x 12	2,400	
Gas & oil	$100 x 12	1,200	
Insurance		1,600	
Licence		75	
Repairs & maintenance		750	6,025
CLOTHING			
Purchases		2,000	
Laundry & dry cleaning	$ 30 x 12	360	2,360
RECREATION, READING, & EDUCATION			
Travel		2,400	
Club memberships		900	
Miscellaneous	$100 x 12	1,200	4,500

TOBACCO & ALCOHOL		–
HEALTH & PERSONAL CARE		
Medicine & medical services		
not covered by insurance	200	
Medical & dental insurance		
premiums, including provincial		
health care	700	
Dental care not covered by		
insurance	400	
Grooming	200	1,500
OTHER		
Gifts to friends & family		500
TOTAL PERSONAL EXPENDITURES		**$28,965**

"Hold on a second, Uncle Bill," I said. "Can I borrow your pencil and a piece of paper?"

With a flourish he handed me his rosewood pencil and I grabbed for the pad on the table.

"So, if I earn $40,000," I said while writing, "and my income taxes work out to be $10,000 and my cost of living is $29,000, that takes $39,000 out of $40,000 and leaves me with only $1,000 in savings for mutual funds. That's depressing. I did a lot better living at home," I wailed.

"Obviously, you did better living at home," said Uncle Bill, "but you can't live at home forever. The only thing is, you're forgetting one important point."

"What's that?"

"Your mortgage principal repayment. Remember, before dinner I showed you how you would be paying off over $19,000 in mortgage principal over the next five years? Now, it's true, in the fourth and fifth years, you'll pay off more than you do in the first, second and third years. But, if we simply average out the $19,000 over five years, for all intents and purposes, your net worth increases by $3,800 a year. What you're therefore doing is putting aside $1,000 in mutual funds and $3,800 in the form of increased equity in your house. That works out as $4,800 in total, which is about 12 per cent of your before-tax earnings. That's not too shabby. In fact, based on what you've jotted down here tonight, and on the assumption you go ahead and buy that house, you should still continue to set aside $300 a month in mutual funds."

"$300 a month?"

"Yes," said Uncle Bill. "Don't forget there's $200 a month going towards the eventual replacement of your car and another $100 a month for long-term savings. If you have to, you can cut back a bit on your miscellaneous entertainment. You've already come to the conclusion on your own that you've got some flexibility there."

LOGAN'S PROJECTED INCREASE IN NET WORTH IN FIRST YEAR LIVING ALONE

Projected income		$40,000
Less: Income taxes (25%)	$ 10,000	
Cost of living	29,000	39,000
Savings for mutual funds investment		1,000
Mortgage principal repayment		3,800
Projected increase in net worth		$ 4,800

"There's one more thing I'd like to do," I said. "And then maybe we'll call it a night—although God knows how I'm going to sleep tonight with all of this house stuff buzzing through my head."

"I'm sure you'll sleep," said Uncle Bill, "but I'm getting a bit tired too. So, what would you like to do?"

"I'd like to take my budget and summarize what it would cost me to live if I just took the easy way out."

"The easy way?"

"Yeah," I said. "If I didn't buy a house and rented instead. In fact, I'd like to see what it would cost even if I didn't spend as much on entertainment."

"I see, " said Uncle Bill. "What you'd like to do is put together a 'bare-bones' budget."

"That's a good way of putting it," I said.

He reached out, took his pencil from my hand, and grabbed for the pad of paper.

"Okay," he said. "Let's just do it."

Uncle Bill jotted down the seven categories off the consumer price index.

141

"Now, for housing," he began, "it's pretty hard today to rent an apartment, anything decent that is, for less than $400 a month including utilities—even if you share. So that's $4,800 a year. For food, even if you eat all your meals at home by yourself, it's pretty difficult to live a healthy lifestyle on less than $50 a week; that's $2,600 a year. Let's see...transportation. Most people your age are going to want cars and they're going to have car payments. They'd have to budget at least $200 a month towards the purchase of a car and their gas, oil, insurance, repairs, etc., wouldn't be any less than yours. So, I think $6,000 a year for transportation is about reasonable."

"That's interesting, Uncle Bill," I interrupted. "It seems it can cost more to own and operate a car than it does to have a place to live."

"That's quite true," he said. "Now, clothing. You budgeted $2,360 for buying clothes, laundry, dry cleaning, and so on. I think someone could probably get by on around $1,400 a year and still not look like a slob; recognizing that one would want to have some decent clothes and one can't live his or her whole life in jeans. For recreation, I think $100 a month is a bare minimum—if someone wants to have at least a little bit of fun. Would you agree?"

"Sounds okay with me, Uncle Bill. Let's add it up."

"Not so fast," he said. "We'll throw in another $1,000 for health and personal care. Let's see, seven numbers.... Even though I'm a chartered accountant, or C.A., which means I 'Can't Add', I think I can handle this without my calculator." He zipped quickly through the numbers. "$17,000."

THE "BARE-BONES" (NO FRILLS) BUDGET

Housing	$400 x 12	$ 4,800
Food	$ 50 x 52	2,600
Transportation		6,000
Clothing		1,400
Recreation	$100 x 12	1,200
Health & Personal Care		1,000
Total		$17,000

"Wow," I said. "That's amazing. It's also scary."

"Why's that?" asked Uncle Bill.

142

"There are so many young people, my peers in fact, who are suffering today working at what you told Andrea and me a number of years ago are 'McJobs', and now I can see why. Even if you earn *double* the minimum wage, $10 an hour, say, 40 hours a week, 50 weeks a year, that's only $20,000 on an annual basis. After taxes, you can barely live! I suppose you can make do if you share your apartment, but now I know why it's so tough out there in the 'real world'."

"You're right about that," said Uncle Bill. "And the sad thing is that if kids today don't learn these facts of life at an early age, they're in for quite a shock down the road."

"But what can they do about it?"

"Basically the same thing you and your sister have done. When I came along, you thought that six or eight years out of high school, you'd have a beautiful home with a Porsche in the driveway."

"I can see now," I interrupted, "that might not have been a realistic expectation."

"For you, it very well might be, because *you* took the steps necessary to make sure you wouldn't be mired down with a McJob. And your sister, by becoming a professional, is well on *her* way towards financial success. She'll be in school a few years longer than you, so she might get a later start than you did on things like buying a house, but in the long-run, my boy, you're going to have to work pretty hard to keep up with her."

"I enjoy a good challenge," I said. "But I still feel sorry for a lot of other people."

"It's up to them to get educated and to keep their heads out of the sand. With a little bit of motivation, there are a lot of young people out there who can learn to nurture their own entrepreneurial talents the way you and Andrea did by learning to *think smart* at an early age. Here you are, just barely 22 years old, and already thinking of becoming a real estate tycoon."

"Thanks to you, Uncle Bill. I'll buy dinner."

"We'll go dutch," replied Uncle Bill reaching for his wallet.

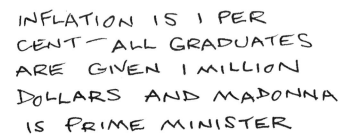

INFLATION IS 1 PER
CENT — ALL GRADUATES
ARE GIVEN 1 MILLION
DOLLARS AND MADONNA
IS PRIME MINISTER

Chapter Eleven
June 2004
Andrea's Story:
With an Eye on the Future

YOU CAN'T IMAGINE how pleased I was that Uncle Bill cut short his annual spring European vacation to return to Canada in time for my graduation from Waterloo as a full-fledged optometrist. Andrea Lavery...Doctor of Optometry. It sounded fantastic to me. Finally, at the age of 24, my school years were behind me and I was free to look towards the future with confidence. It was a sad time, though, because our closely-knit group of 58 students (60 started; only two dropped out) was about to scatter across the continent and beyond. I wondered how long it would be before we would reunite. Two of my classmates who had married each other the previous October were even headed off for a two-year stint in Africa to work for the World Health Organization.

I had opted for a much more conservative approach as the junior member of a three-person team at a large Cyclops Optical branch in my native Ottawa. The starting pay of $34,000 a year was comforting after all these years as a student; although, looking back, I probably could have made about the same money had I continued to teach computer literacy and software programs—stuff I had started to do all those many years ago when I was still in high school and had continued to do to support myself all through my university years. Thank goodness for computers.

With what I was able to earn, I was one of the few students who was able to escape from university without being overburdened by heavy student loans. But I had had enough of teaching software programs and installing systems and I looked forward, with great anticipation, to my new career. I did have a few financial decisions to make and I was really glad Uncle Bill would be around for me to talk to.

As it happened, he came into town a day ahead of the family. When he drove up to the house I had been sharing with three of my classmates for the past two years, he started to apologize and fumbled a bit, pretending that he thought the graduation was the next day and not two days later. Finally he ended up admitting he had come in a day early just to spend some 'quality time' as he put it, before the hordes arrived. Nora had gone to visit her sister in Sarnia, but promised to be back in time for the ceremony.

We had an early dinner because it was obvious Uncle Bill was still somewhat jet-lagged, and we caught up on family gossip. Uncle Bill entertained me with stories of his wanderings with Nora around Northern Italy and Switzerland. I offered to make us both a picnic lunch the next day and suggested we might go for a drive in the country. I knew of a couple of really nice spots and I thought he and I could enjoy the beauty of a late Southern Ontario spring.

Uncle Bill jumped at the idea and we agreed he would pick me up the next morning around 11:00. I went home, packed a picnic lunch and put a nice bottle of Niagara Falls Chardonnay in the fridge to cool overnight. We're not big drinkers in our family, but once in a while, it's nice to share a bottle of wine on a special occasion. I told Uncle Bill I would have to be back home by 4:00 because I had an appointment to get my hair cut at 4:45 the next afternoon. It wasn't something that I treated myself to often, but after all, a girl only becomes a doctor once in her lifetime, doesn't she?

❧

The following day dawned bright and cheerful and by the time noon rolled around, Uncle Bill and I were already settled on our blanket under a huge maple tree at the edge of a lovely meadow. There was a stream a few metres away and I stuck the Chardonnay bottle into the water to keep it cool. I peeled off my shirt and shorts and stretched out in my bathing suit on the blanket. Uncle Bill even removed his shirt revealing a well-tanned and well-proportioned physique for a man nudging 55.

Now, if this sounds like the beginning of a romance novel, let me hasten to tell you 'that's all she wrote', as they say. After all, we are uncle and niece, and Uncle Bill is as innocent as the driven snow. To be honest, my motives weren't quite as pure— although not in the way you might think. I wanted some financial advice and I welcomed the opportunity to use my uncle as a sounding board. I also knew that once he got into financial planning mode, he'd end up having more fun than I would!

But first things first. We ate our tuna fish sandwiches and chewed on carrots, chasing our food down with two glasses each of crisp white wine. I had packed a couple of apples and some chocolate brownies for dessert, but we both decided to take a break from eating after the sandwiches had disappeared.

Finally, Uncle Bill stretched out and said, "Well young lady, what's on your mind?"

"What do you mean, Uncle Bill?" I asked puzzled.

"I'm sure," said Uncle Bill dryly, "that on this day before your graduation you could have had your choice of literally dozens of good-looking young men to take with you on this wonderful picnic and yet you chose me. Surely you have an ulterior motive."

I could see Uncle Bill was kidding me and I rushed to assure him that, of all the people I knew, there was nobody with whom I would rather spend this lovely day.

"But," I said, "now that you mention it, there are a couple of things I would like to talk to you about."

"Ah ha," said Uncle Bill, "now we come to your ulterior motive." I felt myself blush and then began to relax as I could see my uncle was enjoying pulling my leg.

"I need your advice," I began, "on a whole bunch of things."

"Fire away," said Uncle Bill with glee, "that's what I'm here for. Besides, I have to earn my lunch, don't I?" He laughed.

"Okay," I said. "Well, first of all, I hope you're not disappointed in me."

"Why should I be?"

"The fact that I decided to take the job with Cyclops Optical instead of going into my own practice. There are about five or six of my classmates who've decided to open up their own shops right away but I wasn't one of them...I hope you don't think any less of me."

"Now, don't be silly," said Uncle Bill. "Why should I think any less of you?"

"Because you've always tried to influence Logan and me to become entrepreneurs."

"That's true," said Uncle Bill, "but that's in the long-run. You're not exactly over the hill at the age of 25."

"24," I corrected.

Uncle Bill nodded. "As far as I'm concerned, the best thing you can do is spend a few years working for Cyclops Optical."

"Really?" I said.

"Yup," said Uncle Bill. "You know, I used to teach in the accountancy program, first in Montreal and then later on in Calgary after I moved to Alberta in the late '70s. I remember telling my students the worst thing they could do was leave the cocoon of chartered accountancy firms too quickly after they finished their exams just because they might earn a couple of thousand dollars more. I would tell them how, in the year or two following graduation, they could learn more by staying with a larger firm than they had learned all the way through their academic programs."

"Why's that, Uncle Bill?"

"It's because when you don't have the pressure of writing exams, your mind is clear and you can learn how business really operates. In your case, you know all the up-to-date methods of doing eye examinations. But what do you really know about operating an optometry practice? Do you know whether to buy your equipment or lease it? How do you select space in a building and, more importantly, where should you be locating? What do you know about hiring staff? An optician or two, a receptionist... Even though you've been quite successful at earning money from your computer teaching, how much do you really know about advertising or setting up a proper accounting system and billing procedures?"

I could feel myself deflating as Uncle Bill hammered me with all the many things I had never thought about in the practice of optometry. He was a good judge of my body language though and he quickly reached out and grabbed me gently by the shoulder.

"But don't worry," he continued, "all of this will fall into place at the right time. You're a lot better off over the next few years working for someone else and learning all the best procedures. If you want to stay in the Ottawa area, you can keep your eyes open for a good location. You may decide, in the final analysis, that you're actually happy working for a big company and, if so, there's no law that says you have to be an entrepreneur. You weren't put on earth to please your Uncle Bill. You've got to please yourself. You may also decide you'd rather join a partnership than practice on your own. There isn't any rush. Keep your options flexible. In the meantime, you're free from university examinations so you've got much more opportunity to learn how business works. Pay special attention to the administrative facets of an optometry practice and then, if you do decide to go on your own, you'll know what you're doing and you won't make any serious mistakes." He paused, took a deep breath and continued.

"You have to wait until you're ready. I didn't go out on my own as an independent tax consultant until I was 33. And, at that time, I had a wife and kids to support and I remember thinking long and hard before taking the plunge. Today, I look back and sometimes I say to myself 'why didn't I do this five years earlier?' I really didn't learn all that much between my late 20s and early 30s working for somebody else. But the plain truth was, I wasn't ready. So you can't rush it."

"Well, at least you made up for lost time, Uncle Bill. You certainly did quite well for yourself."

"That's true," said Uncle Bill proudly. "And you'll do fine yourself. So, for now, concentrate on doing the best job you can. Enjoy the fact that you're going to be getting a regular paycheque and make sure you put some of it away."

"That's another point, Uncle Bill. I really don't want to disappoint you, but right now I just don't want to be like Logan."

"In what way?"

"Well, remember two or three years ago, you advised him to buy a house instead of renting?... Now he's happier than the proverbial pig. You should see him rave on about Uncle Bill and his great advice. He's especially happy because the Ottawa real estate market has gained almost 20 per cent in the last few years. But," I wailed, "I just don't want to buy a house. And again, I'm afraid you're going to be disappointed in me."

"There's no need for you to buy a house right now, Andrea," said Uncle Bill. "You're not settled yet. Logan seems pretty clear he wants to stay in Ottawa. Now, of course, things can change and you never know where you're going to wind up even a few years down the road. But for you, the world is your oyster, so to speak. After the next couple of years, you could conceivably go into a practice anywhere in North America, or abroad for that matter. And you might not want to be saddled with a house you'd have to sell at whatever the market would bear at that particular time just so you could get some money out and move on to wherever you're going. You've got ample opportunity to buy a house later on. For now, if you're more comfortable renting, by all means do so."

"So you're not disappointed?"

"No, of course not, my dear. I understand. Buying a house isn't for everyone. Your profession is secure and your income is likely to go up over time so you can always buy a house later on."

"But what if it costs much more then?"

"Well, that's the chance you have to take. And that's why it's so important for you to make sure you have an investment program from which you can draw your downpayment if and when the time comes."

All of a sudden Uncle Bill stopped cold as he saw my face drop. "What's the matter, dear?" he asked.

"Well," I said, "I might as well confess."

Uncle Bill waited patiently as I hesitated.

"As you know, I've followed your advice and bought mutual funds with my earnings. In fact, while I lived at home during my undergraduate years I was not only able to pay my tuition fees and cover book costs and so on, I even saved some money. In the last three years, even though I wasn't able to put anything aside, I never had to dip into my savings. In other words, what I earned covered my tuition, books and living expenses here in Waterloo."

"So, I don't understand," said Uncle Bill. "You haven't been able to save money over the last three years while in optometry school. Big deal. You've still got good habits and you've got a nest egg. I don't see the problem."

"Well, hang on, Uncle Bill. I'm getting there," I said a bit petulantly. "Counting appreciation, by last September, I had just over $20,000 invested."

"And..."

"And then I started dating this guy in the business faculty who dabbled in the stock market."

"Uh, oh," said Uncle Bill.

"I suppose you can see what's coming. He told me about this mining stock he was following on the Vancouver Stock Exchange and how he figured it would triple in the next year."

"You didn't..."

"Well, it may not be quite as bad as you think. I surely didn't take the whole $20,000 but I did take a quarter of my savings...."

"$5,000?"

I nodded.

"And threw that, as it were, down the toilet." Uncle Bill sighed deeply. "That's an expensive lesson you learned, my dear. But better earlier than later. Once in a while, stock tips pan out and, if the truth be told, if you have inside information on a company you can make a lot of money. Many years ago, before I went into tax practice on a full-time basis, I worked for an accounting firm that had a couple of clients that were junior industrial stocks listed on the Montreal Stock Exchange. Unfortunately, accountants aren't allowed to buy shares in the companies they audit."

"Why's that, Uncle Bill?"

"I guess it's because the governing body, The Institute of Chartered Accountants, feels that if their members were allowed

BUY GOLD

Wicks

to buy
stocks in their clients' companies, this
could influence the accuracy of the
financial statements."

"You mean an accountant might falsify figures just to make
the stock price go up?"

"I'm sure that wouldn't happen too often, but even once
would be too much," said Uncle Bill. "Anyway, I remember doing
the audit of these junior industrials and being among the first
to know the actual profit levels. Had I bought stock, I could have
made a fair amount of money, although, in those days, I didn't

have that much to invest. But I learned a valuable lesson and that is: *it's the insiders who make money on individual stocks, not the so-called 'man in the street'.* That's why I recommend mutual funds.... You get two things...."

"I know," I interrupted dejectedly, "professional money-management and a chance to hedge your bets."

"Bang on," said Uncle Bill. "But one mistake isn't the end of the world. You've still got $15,000 left."

"True, but I want to buy a car. You remember back when I was in second year I bought Mom's old car from her?"

"Yes, I do," Uncle Bill said. "You've still got that old beater?"

"That's the whole point. Not only has it pretty well rusted out, but the repairs are starting to get out of hand."

"So, go ahead, buy a car. You're no longer a poor starving student."

"But if I use up my $15,000 to buy a car now, I won't have anything left."

"How much do you need?"

"Well," I said, "I can probably get a decent car for my purposes for about $12,000 but then I also need around $3,000 for other stuff. I've got an apartment lined up not too far from work and I need some furniture. Fortunately, I've managed to accumulate quite a bit over the last few years and I don't need that much."

"But you won't be comfortable if you spend all your savings, will you?" asked Uncle Bill.

I nodded my head dejectedly.

"You know," he said, "your financial position is certainly not bad. After all, here you are a Doctor of Optometry and you don't even have student loans to worry about. Actually, in your case, I wouldn't recommend selling your mutuals. How have they performed for you?"

"Well, my average return has been about 14 per cent a year." Uncle Bill reached in to his pocket and pulled out a calculator. My eyebrows raised in surprise.

"Old habits die hard," he said. "I didn't bring my copy of Zimmer's *'Money Manager'* with me but this little baby here will do the trick. I picked it up in Switzerland last week. It's not on the North American market yet. Cost me almost as much in duty and GST to bring it in as it cost me to buy it. Watch this." He pressed a couple of buttons.

"Wie viel hast du investiert?" asked the calculator in German.

"Whoops," he said, "I forgot to change the language." He pressed another button.

"How much do you have invested?" the calculator asked in English.

"$15,000."

"$15,000," repeated the calculator. "What is the anticipated annual return?"

"14 per cent."

"14 per cent," repeated the calculator. "What is the length of time that the money will be invested?" asked the calculator.

"40 years."

"40 years," repeated the calculator. "One moment please...At the end of 40 years, you will have $2,833,260. Do you wish to have this converted to Deutschmarks?"

"No, thank you, it will not be necessary."

"Did I hear right, Uncle Bill?"

"Apparently so," my uncle responded. "I can always check this with the *Money Manager* book, but it seems that $15,000 left alone to earn 14 per cent growth over the next 40 years will amount to $2.8 million."

"So what do I do? I sure don't want to give that up," I said.

"You don't have to, Andrea. What I suggest you do is use a little bit of leverage."

"Huh?" I asked.

Uncle Bill smiled.

"I remember explaining the concept to Logan a couple of years ago, although in his case, the circumstances were different. Leverage basically means *borrowing against what you've got* in order to expand your capital base *without selling what you've got.*"

"I'm not sure I understand."

"I'll make it simple for you," replied Uncle Bill. "You've got $15,000 in mutual funds that are growing at the rate of 14 per cent a year."

I nodded.

"There's nothing to stop you from going to a financial institution and borrowing $15,000 using your mutual funds as collateral. The fact that you have collateral in the form of marketable securities, along with a profession and a good-paying job means you should be able to borrow money at probably not more than prime plus two per cent. And that's about an eight per cent annual cost, at least today."

"I get it," I said. "There's no point in me giving up investments that yield 14 per cent when I can borrow money at eight per cent."

"Exactly. Although, in theory, you could get into trouble if your mutual funds suddenly declined in value."

My spirits sank.

"But in your case, you'd be borrowing for a relatively short period. Based on your income, you should be able to pay off $15,000 over three, or at the most four, years. Probably three years will do," he said, nodding his head as he did some mental arithmetic.

"I get it," I said. "I use my earnings from my job to pay off the debt and I keep my investments intact."

"That's right. And remember, against your debt you'll also have a car and furniture. True, they'll depreciate, but even at the end of three years a $12,000 car will probably be worth at least $6,000 or $7,000."

"So I hang on to my investments, and I use my income from my job..."

"That's right, your cash flow," interrupted Uncle Bill.

"...I use my cash flow," I continued, "to subsidize my debt."

"You've got it! *There's nothing wrong with incurring some debt as long as you have assets to support your debt and an income with which to pay it off.*"

"And I qualify on both counts."

"So you do."

"And, psychologically," I said, "I'm a lot happier because I still have my investments."

"Right. Now this isn't the time or place to do it, but I think you and I should sit down and prepare a budget."

155

"I remember you did that with Logan. And actually, I don't have to burden you with that. I can get the blank form from him. He explained what I need to do."

"Okay," said Uncle Bill, "you tell me."

"Well, first I have to calculate what my take-home pay is going to be, and I've already done that. It's a little over $22,000 a year. So, if my rent, including utilities, is about $600 a month and I take $400 a month to pay off my loan for the car and furniture, that still leaves me over $10,000 a year for food, clothing, car expenses, and entertainment. I've pretty well calculated that these costs shouldn't run more than about $7,000 or $8,000 a year, so I should be okay."

"You've got a good head for numbers," said Uncle Bill nodding approvingly. "The country lost a good accountant when you decided to become an optometrist."

I sniffed haughtily.

"I know, I know, no glamour in accounting," said Uncle Bill. "Anyhow, it seems as if you're in good shape. If you can save $2,000 a year over and above your loan payments, you're not doing too badly."

"Actually," I said, "I think I can do a little better. Although I do want to devote most of my time to my career, computers are still my hobby and I figure I can earn another couple of thousand dollars a year even if I scale down my course-teaching substantially. Then again, with machines like the one you've just shown me, I wonder how long it'll be before these guys run themselves."

We both looked down at Uncle Bill's calculator.

"Yes, technology sure is amazing," said Uncle Bill, "but, for the next few years, I don't think you've got a lot to worry about."

"The bottom line," I said, "is that, if I can make another couple of thousand dollars a year teaching, even after taxes, my total savings should come to around $3,000 a year."

"That's not bad at all," said Uncle Bill. "If you can save 10 per cent of your income and add that to your capital, you'll be a wealthy lady long before age 65. There's quite a benefit in starting early."

"I just have to be careful with these babies over here," I said, sticking my hand into my purse and pulling out three brightly coloured credit cards.

"Holy smokes," said Uncle Bill, "where did you get those?"

"It's amazing," I answered. "I guess the various credit card companies find out from the universities who's about to graduate and then they send you these cards, along with fancy brochures outlining all the benefits. No wonder credit card interest rates are so high. It's amazing what they spend on advertising."

Uncle Bill shook his head. "Credit cards are one of the biggest problems we face in this country because most people don't know how to use them."

"How so?"

"Like everything else in the investment game, my dear, credit cards require discipline. I use them all the time, but I use them properly. They're great to have if you don't want to carry a whole lot of cash with you. But the important point is *never put something on a credit card unless you'll be able to pay your bill in full at the end of the month*. Nora and I travel and eat out a lot," he continued, "and we probably put as much as $1,500 a month on our cards."

I whistled in surprise.

"Now put this into perspective," he said. "I'm not poor, as you know, and neither is Nora, and I suppose we deserve the privilege of being able to travel and eat out when we want, although I do concede, in the eyes of many people, we probably live a pretty extravagant lifestyle. Anyway," he said, "the amount we put on our credit cards is not really the point at issue. What I'm trying to say is we would *never* put a purchase on a card if we didn't know we could pay the bill in full at the end of the month."

"Is it because of the high interest rates?"

"Yes, in part," said Uncle Bill. "It's expensive financing if you're paying off your credit cards over time. But it's more than that. If people don't use their credit responsibly, they end up building up their credit card limits to the maximum. Sometimes, you'll even find that a card issued to you has a relatively low credit limit and, when you build your debt up, instead of putting on the brakes, the credit card company simply increases your limit. They're happy if you owe them $3,000, $5,000 or even $10,000—as long as you eventually pay. But if you get stuck having bought things you can't afford and you have to dread picking up the mail every day, you're certainly not going to get ahead financially. Many people are so heavily in hock on their credit cards, they're constantly depressed about their finances. In fact, they're so depressed they're immobilized. How can you start putting money away for retirement or a rainy day when you don't even start with a clean slate?"

I looked puzzled.

"What I mean by that," said Uncle Bill, "is, if you owe $10,000 and you know it's going to take you three or four years to pay that off, how can you even *begin* to think about a savings and investment program? Many people just give up. They pay down their credit cards, and then build up their balances again, and so it goes and eventually they run out of time. Credit cards are like having a loaded gun. Now, if your hobby is hunting, for example—which doesn't turn my crank by the way—a gun can be extremely useful. But you have to respect guns because they can also be extremely dangerous."

"Maybe people should be licensed to hold credit cards the same way they have licences for firearms," I said.

"That's probably not such a bad idea," said Uncle Bill nodding. "You were probably half-joking when you suggested it, but it sure makes sense to me. If we're to prosper as a country, we have to do everything we can to do away with the irresponsible use of credit cards. And the right place to start is in the school system."

"It's actually starting to happen, Uncle Bill," I said. "I read an article in the Times-Herald a couple of weekends ago..."

"Your old newspaper?"

"Yes, 'my' newspaper, the one that got Logan and me started. Anyway, I read this article that said the high schools were starting to give classes in credit card management as part of their health and lifestyles programs."

"I guess I won't have to write to Prime Minister Cormack

after all," said Uncle Bill.

"Probably not."

"There's one more thing I wanted to talk to you about, young lady," Uncle Bill continued.

"How about some dessert first?" I asked. "Would you like an apple or a chocolate brownie?"

"You really think you have to ask?" replied Uncle Bill. "I know what I *should* have but I'll go for the brownie. After all, you can't always do what's good for you and chocolate is such sweet surrender."

CHAPTER TWELVE

ANDREA'S STORY CONTINUED: THE REGISTERED RETIREMENT SAVINGS PLAN—AN IMPORTANT CORNERSTONE OF CANADIAN FINANCIAL PLANNING

IN SHORT ORDER, Uncle Bill polished off both brownies, his and mine, so I retaliated by eating both apples. We washed our food down with the last half-glass each of cold wine and I packed up the dregs of our meal to take back with us for recycling back home. Uncle Bill stretched out on the blanket, rubbed his eyes, and looked at his watch.

"Well," he said, "we still have a bit of time before we have to start heading back so you can get to your beauty appointment on time—not that you need it, my dear," he added gallantly. "And there's one other thing I want to talk to you about. It's the Registered Retirement Savings Plan—or RRSP—a very important cornerstone to your financial security." He paused for a moment at the puzzled look on my face. "Do you know how these things work?"

"I know something about them," I said, "but not a whole lot. I know there's all these ads about RRSPs in January and February. Then, after the tax deadline on them is over, I hear nothing about them. I know they offer some tax benefits, but I've never paid much attention because I wasn't earning that much money anyhow. Then again, I'm going to be earning some decent coin starting soon..." I said, as comprehension slowly began to sink in.

Uncle Bill nodded, as if he could see the light bulb going on in my head. "I won't bore you with all the gruesome details, but basically, here's the deal," he began. "The government encourages Canadians to save for their own retirements by offering a formula for saving."

"Sort of like a pension plan at work?"

Uncle Bill nodded. "Are you going to be part of the Cyclops pension?"

"Not for the first two years," I said. "They told me that, for administrative purposes, they don't bring new employees in until they've completed two years of service."

"That's probably smart," said Uncle Bill, "from their point of view. I'm sure a good deal of their staff turnover takes place relatively early on. If you're still with them in a couple of years, we'll cross that bridge when we get to it. If you're lucky, they'll get rid of their plan."

"Why's that?"

"Because the way economics and business have gone, I wouldn't put my faith in a workplace, or for that matter government, pension plan. Most people just sign the pension papers when they begin their jobs and never read the fine print until it's too late."

"You know Mom's friend, Nancy Rosenburg?"

"I've met her," said Uncle Bill.

"When her husband died, she received widow's benefits from his pension. She was telling Mom that she gave the money to her son for university. Then she remarried and was cut off."

"An excellent example," Uncle Bill said. "Consider all the companies that have moved their head offices to other countries with different pension regulations and have forced their Canadian employees to take early retirement."

"Gee, I remember a few years ago reading about some big corporate boss in Toronto who took the excess earnings from a pension fund and put them into his own company's operating funds," I recalled. "There was quite a scandal."

"There are lots of these stories," Uncle Bill said. "The key is, I wouldn't get emotionally or psychologically attached to any security-from-a-workplace pension. Friends of mine in Alberta participated in a teachers' pension that was technically bankrupt in the '80s because the provincial government, which ran the plan, mismanaged it. I'm much happier with RRSPs."

"You can concentrate on your own efforts," I said.

"Exactly," Uncle Bill nodded. "Each year, you can put up to 18 per cent of your *previous year's earned income* into an RRSP program. Whatever you contribute is tax-deductible. Now, for this year there isn't much point in contributing, but you should start thinking about next year. If you earn, say, $17,000 over the rest of this year, 18 per cent of that is around $3,000. You'll be able to put that money in for a tax deduction *next year*."

"That's what confuses me the most about RRSPs, Uncle Bill," I said. "I'm not sure what tax-deductible is. I mean is it something that reduces the amount on which we pay taxes each year? My friend, the same guy that got me into that stock market fiasco, told me we only get tax credits."

"Most of what used to be deductions are now tax credits— the better for the tax collector to bite you with, my dear," Uncle Bill said with a leer. "But RRSP contributions are still direct deductions with qualifications. They're actually more like tax deferrals."

"You've lost me, Uncle Bill," I said.

"Hang on and it'll all come clear. The combined federal and provincial tax rate in this country on incomes greater than $30,000 a year averages around 40 per cent. Remember I showed that to you way back when, I guess it must be almost 10 years ago?"

"I remember," I said. "And for higher income people, the top rate goes to 50 per cent or more."

"You've got a good memory," said Uncle Bill. "By next year, let's assume you're earning $36,000. If you contribute $3,000 to an RRSP, in other words 18 per cent of *this year's* earned income, you'll be in a 40 per cent tax bracket. When you deduct the $3,000 off your gross earnings when you do your tax return, you'll save 40 cents on the dollar. In other words, when the smoke clears, the government will absorb 40 per cent of your

$3,000 in the form of an income tax refund and it'll only cost you 60 per cent."

"You mean it'll only cost me $1,800 to have $3,000 working for me?"

"That's right," said Uncle Bill.

"You mean I'll get a tax refund at the end of the year?"

"Or, if you continue to moonlight, like you said you would, and do a bit of computer teaching to make some extra money, you won't have to send in any taxes at the end. Also," Uncle Bill continued, "remember a couple of minutes ago, you talked about the RRSP advertising in January and February? Most people wait until the last minute to make their contributions for the previous year because the government lets you have until March 1, each year, to contribute for the previous year ended December 31."

"What's wrong with waiting?" I asked.

"Two things. First, many people find they don't have the money in one lump-sum at the end, so they miss out on making their contributions. Also, even if most people were like you and

164

had the discipline to save, they'd be better off contributing throughout the year, rather than waiting for the end."

"That's because they'd be earning compound income starting earlier, is that right?"

"Bang on again, my dear," said Uncle Bill.

"But what is the real benefit of an RRSP compared to my mutual fund investments? I mean, on my mutuals, I'm earning growth at 14 per cent."

"You can make the same mutual fund investments using an RRSP," said Uncle Bill.

"So why bother? I don't understand."

Uncle Bill frowned. "I'm sure if you try you can figure it out."

I thought for a moment. "Of course, you're right. I've got it. Right now, when I've been buying mutual funds all along, it's been with money that I earned that I really didn't have to pay any tax on. Because of my personal tax credits and claims for tuition fees and so on, I was never taxable, so whatever I invested was tax-paid money that the government never took any part of."

"And..." prodded Uncle Bill.

"And now I'm going to be earning taxable income, and for me to invest money from here on in, outside of an RRSP, means I'm going to have to give the government 40 cents out of each dollar first; which means I'm better off with an RRSP mutual fund where I can invest 100 cents out of each \$1 instead of only 60 cents on the \$1 outside."

"Exactly," said Uncle Bill.

"So should I switch everything into RRSPs from here on in? My whole focus?" I asked.

"For a while, anyway," said Uncle Bill. "You may as well maximize your RRSPs. *If you earn more than \$30,000 a year, it's only when you're able to save money over and above 18 per cent of your earnings that you should look at unsheltered investments,* meaning investments made with *after-tax* dollars, and, for most people, that doesn't happen until way down the line."

"Why's that?"

"Well, for most people, like your brother, there's the

advantage of buying a house and paying for it. So, if *you* wanted to buy a house *and* contribute to an RRSP you'd have your hands full for quite a number of years. Once your house was paid and you were living more or less rent-free, ignoring taxes and utilities, then, if you're earning lots of money and can afford to save more than 18 per cent of your earnings, you'd put the extra amount of after-tax dollars into *unsheltered* investments. But, for now, your focus over the next few years should be on an RRSP."

"So if you were giving advice to young people..."

"You're not so old, my dear."

"No, I mean teenagers—'yo-ads'."

"I'd suggest the exact same direction I gave you. If you earn income on a part-time basis while you're in high school or university and you can afford to save, I'd suggest the same mutual fund program I recommended to you because your earnings weren't high enough to be taxed in the first place. So, in that situation, there really isn't a whole lot of point in buying an RRSP. Then, once you have a full-time job and start to earn more than $30,000, it pays to switch over your *future* mutual funds investments to an RRSP because the government will start to subsidize 40 cents out of each $1 that you invest."

"There's got to be a catch, though. How does that work?"

"There's no catch," said Uncle Bill, "but here's what happens. You start to contribute into an RRSP and each year the value of your investments grows and you continue to add more. Ultimately, you'll have a huge pool of retirement capital. In your case, if you start now, and put aside $3,000 a year, in monthly payments for the next 40 years or so until you're 65, you'll have an astronomical amount of money, assuming you earn 12 per cent on average each year."

"How much do you think I'll have?"

"Let's ask my new computer," said Uncle Bill. He punched in the numbers and asked the question.

"$3,000 a year in equal monthly payments of $250, yielding 12 per cent per annum, for 40 years will amount to $2,941,193." We both looked at the little machine. Uncle Bill quickly punched the recall button.

166

"Repeat. $2,941,193."

"I don't believe it," I said.

"Frankly, I have trouble believing it myself," said Uncle Bill, "although I think our little friend here is right. After all, the Germans do provide a five-year warranty. I can check with '*The Money Manager*' when I get home, but I remember when we talked 10 years ago about putting aside $200 a month, we were well into the millions by the time you reached age 65."

"Then why isn't everybody rich?" I asked.

"People are too busy living from day to day to think about the future," said Uncle Bill. "It's not that difficult, as you yourself have already discovered. You don't have to sacrifice all that much to put aside savings. The peace of mind you get is worth a lot more than the odd movie or dinner you might have to forgo."

"That's true, Uncle Bill. When I was a kid, I didn't waste my money in the arcades playing computer games. I could get the same enjoyment at home playing Nintendo. So what happens at the end? You didn't answer my question."

"Well, let's assume you have around $3 million at the end. What happens is that, at some point, no later than your age 71, you must start to draw the money out and you have to pay tax on your withdrawals."

"Ah ha, the government does get its pound of flesh!"

"True, you'll have to pay tax and you obviously aren't going to be in a lower tax-bracket after you retire than before. In fact, people talk about going into lower brackets after retirement, but that's not something *I* would ever want to happen to *me*."

"I see your point, Uncle Bill. The lower your tax-bracket, the less you're earning."

"Exactly. Now it's true, people can usually afford to live on less after they retire because their houses should be paid for and their kids are grown up. They also may not need as much in the way of clothes if they're not going to work any more. But if you stop to think about it, why should you have less after you retire than before? You've got all this wonderful vacation time, why not have the money to enjoy it?"

"Like you do," I said.

"Exactly. It's nice to go to Europe every year in May before all the tourists start converging on the continent and it's darn nice to spend a month in the Caribbean when the Canadian winters get a little bit too much to take. Then there's the house in Phoenix..."

"You've got me convinced, Uncle Bill. For this year, I'll have to concentrate on paying off my car and furniture loan but I should still have some money left over for investment."

"Probably $1,000 or so, but you'd be well advised to..."

"I know, continue to have the money deducted off my bank account on a regular basis as my paycheque comes in."

"You're a good study, Andrea. I'm proud of you. I never have to tell you the same thing twice. Sounds like there's a lot of new things *you* can tell *me*." Uncle Bill shrugged modestly.

"Now, are there other options besides growth mutual funds for RRSP investments?"

"Oh, there's lots of alternatives, although there are some restrictions. For example, you can't buy real estate or gold and other precious metals and only up to 20 per cent can be invested in foreign securities. But in the same way as there are many kinds of mutual funds beyond growth funds, there are also a lot of RRSP alternatives."

"For instance?"

"You can put your money into term deposits, guaranteed investment certificates, bonds, mortgages and so on. You can even lend yourself money to buy a home, although the actual procedure is a bit complicated."

"So, why aren't you recommending some of these choices instead?"

"If you were 44 years old and not 24, I would. Generally, if a person is in a 40 per cent tax bracket or higher, I don't recommend that he or she earn interest outside an RRSP because, at today's interest rates, it doesn't pay. But within the RRSP, it's a different story. If you earn, say, six or seven per cent in an RRSP where your ongoing income is not taxed, your gross yield and your net yield are the same..."

"As long as you don't take it out."

"Yes, as long as you don't take it out. You get the benefit of compounding on a pre-tax, not after-tax, basis."

"But why aren't you recommending this for me?"

"Well, in your case, at your age, you can afford to take a little bit of risk for the extra return. You see, we hope that *your* mutual funds will generate anywhere from 10 to 14 per cent average annual growth. If you have one bad year, like the crash of '99..."

"I remember," I said. "Both Logan and I lost money on our investments that year."

"Exactly, but did it matter in the long run?"

"No, the following year we both got better than 20 per cent."

"And at your ages, you could afford to take the chance. The older you are, the fewer chances you want to take. In my case, I'm not looking for the same 14 per cent returns that I'm suggesting for you. And my RRSPs are therefore invested in interest-bearing funds, including mortgage funds. I'm content to earn seven or eight per cent each year. I suppose part of it is because I have other investments as well and am financially secure. But even if I were still working and my only major source of savings was RRSPs, I'd go for the risk-free situation. Then again, I'm 55 while you're not yet 25."

"So, the whole purpose of an RRSP is to have money available *when* you need it to cover your living expenses. I see, though, if I start soon, like next year the way you suggest, my income isn't going to be any lower after retirement than before. Do you think there's any chance, though, that taxes will be less for seniors by the time I get to be one? Shouldn't the government reward people who've saved for their own retirements?"

"Now don't go suggesting governments are going to be any less irresponsible, money-hungry, economic opportunists in the future than what they are now, no matter what our new Prime Minister is up to," Uncle Bill grumbled.

"Such talk, Uncle Bill," I said.

"Well, I've watched for years as these politicians have mismanaged the country to create advantages for their corporate friends at our expense and told us that we demand too much from the government," he growled. "More to the point, what they do is buy votes by spending money the country can't afford and our beautiful country is in economic, emotional and spiritual chaos because of those fools."

"I can see now why you decided to provide for yourself, Uncle Bill," I said. "You don't trust politicians. That's why you used what the system offered to build your *own* security; and now Logan and I are doing the same."

"I've never trusted politicians, my dear," Uncle Bill grumbled. "Anyone who offers to give you a better life by picking your pocket should be shown the door at the end of your foot." He paused. "I never stop hoping we could get an honest one or two in Ottawa because I do believe in a caring society, but when the politicians are cynical power-mongers... Imagine how much better off we'd be without their interference."

"How's your blood pressure?" I asked pointedly.

Uncle Bill glared fiercely for a moment, then laughed. "You're right," he chuckled, then tapped his cheek for a moment as he recollected his thoughts. "We'll just get back to *your* planning and we won't try to cure the ills of the nation in one afternoon. You've got the idea so far, don't you?"

"Yes," I said. "The object of the exercise, as I understand it, is for me to *trade my earnings today for future income.* The way you've explained it to me, RRSPs are quite straightforward. In fact, it seems like a pretty simple and conservative approach to saving."

"You got it," Uncle Bill nodded. "Get rich slow. In fact, if you have, as our little friend here says, almost $3 million by age 65, you'd probably have almost $1 million by the time you're age 55. By starting early, you'll be able to get something most people can't achieve."

"I guess I've really got it made, Uncle Bill. I've got my education, a good career is opening up for me and I have a financial plan. It's funny. This afternoon I was all concerned about having to sell my investments to get some furniture and buy a car and now, just a couple of hours later, all's well with the world."

"That's right," said Uncle Bill. "You've set some goals, short-term and long-term. Your short-term goals are your new car, your furniture, and your job. The long-term goals are, perhaps, to own your own practice some day, and to build financial security. And you've set a plan in motion. As long as you follow that plan and you know where you're going, it isn't going to be too hard to get there."

"But I never would've thought of keeping my investments because they're growing at 14 per cent and borrowing money at only eight per cent to buy what I need."

"True," said Uncle Bill. "It doesn't hurt to have someone show you the way and explore alternatives with you. If I wasn't around, I suppose you could have gone to a reputable financial planner and paid $100 or so for an hour of his or her time. As long as it isn't your friend, 'he-of-the-famous-stock-market-tip'. Well, at least now you know better. A proper plan is one where you get rich *slowly*. From time to time, my dear, you're going to run into people who have made it very quickly. They've been lucky *their* stock tips have panned out for them. But I can guarantee you that a good percentage of the time, these same people who have it made one year will be broke five years later. In the long-run, *you're* the one who's going to be laughing."

"And, in the meantime, I intend to have plenty of fun along the way."

"I'm sure you will," said Uncle Bill looking at his watch. "We'd better get going so you won't be late for your appointment. So tell me about your new car. What are you going to get? I'd like to hear all about Andrea's fabulous dream-machine."

Chapter Thirteen
April 2006
Logan's Story: Trading Up

I<small>T WAS A FINE SPRING DAY</small> in the Nation's capital, but I really wasn't in any mood to enjoy the sunshine glinting off the rapidly-melting snow. I had a tough decision to make and although I'm normally a pretty laid-back type of guy, I was feeling the stress. It was difficult for me to concentrate on my work and I must confess I barked at one of our newer employees who hadn't been pulling his weight. Sometimes decision-making can be tough and it's hard to do when you're distracted by all the normal pressures of day-to-day living. Shortly after lunch, however, the obvious answer popped right into my head. I didn't have to make any decision in a vacuum. I could bounce some ideas off Uncle Bill.

I turned to my phone and punched in his remote accessibility code. It was a neat system that the telephone company had put in two years before. I don't understand all the mechanics of it, but it goes something like this. For $10 a month, you get this gizmo you attach to your key chain. If you keep it activated and someone phones your special number, automatically the phone nearest to where you're standing or sitting will begin to ring. It works fine if you're at home, in your office, or car but it can be rather amusing if two people passing each other get calls at the same time as they pass a phone. Usually, it's not a problem because your key ring attachment starts to beep at the same time the phone rings. So, unless two people meeting at random actually get calls simultaneously, the right person knows to go to the phone. Anyway, I caught Uncle Bill at home packing for his and Nora's annual European jaunt: destination Yugoslavia and Romania. According to the papers, the rebuilt cities in these countries were quite a wonder to behold, although they said the food was still nothing to write home about.

Once I explained there were a couple of things on my mind, Uncle Bill invited me to come over that night after dinner. We exchanged pleasantries, got off the phone and I went back to work. I had a productive afternoon. It's amazing what you can accomplish with a bit of peace of mind.

❧

"Come in, my boy," said Uncle Bill as he let me into his apartment and led me to his spacious living room. "Can I get you a drink? Coffee? Beer?"

"I'll have a beer, Uncle Bill. I had Chinese food for supper and I'm still thirsty."

"Molbatt okay?"

"Fine with me," I said.

Uncle Bill went into his kitchen and returned with two metallized plastic beer bags. I couldn't help but laugh. I could see getting rid of reusable bottles but beer bags—it boggles the mind. Beer just isn't beer if it comes in anything other than a bottle or can—even the new self-crushing cans, no matter how strong the public's commitment to recycling. Molbatt had lost so much money on the beer bags that its share price was only half of what it was three years before when the two predecessor breweries merged.

I settled down in a comfortable chair and looked at my Uncle Bill appraisingly. Uncle Bill was in his mid-50s and the years had been good to him. He still had most of his hair, black, flecked with grey, and a bushy black moustache that seemed to spill over his lower lip. He exercised regularly, and with the amount of travelling he did, sported a perpetual tan.

"So, what's on your mind?" he said. "Let's see, it's been over 10 years now since we started having these little fire-side chats."

"Fire-side?"

"Speaking figuratively, Logan. The 'thought police' from the Ministries of Nature, Preservation, Resource Conservation and Environment would have us in chains in minutes if we had a real wood fire going."

He stopped speaking and for a moment I could see the nostalgia and the yearning for his youth and an open fire cross his face. Well, a middle-aged man's yearning is part of the price we have to pay for the pollution of water and air and the depletion of our woodlands. The price is too high all around. The atmosphere is a mess; our forests are a national disgrace; and emphysema and other non-cancer related respiratory ailments have already surpassed cancer as a cause of death.

Uncle Bill absently reached for the house remote control and punched a button. The big painting on the wall across from his couch, a cowboy theme which he said reminded him of his beloved Alberta, faded to black. It was one of the first of the Thinitron screens invented by Black and General Electronics to be installed in Ottawa. It was a wide screen, home theatre unit in what looked like a portrait frame which now showed a camp scene, an evening on the prairies with a roaring campfire. It was so realistic, I thought I smelled wood smoke; I found out later Uncle Bill had recently bought the Aromatizer option for the system. Uncle Bill watched the fire burn for a few minutes, sighed and turned back to me. "So, what's on your mind? You sounded a bit perplexed this afternoon."

"Well, first of all," I said, "I've got good news. Colleen and I are getting married."

"Congratulations, my boy. I kind of expected that she'd be the one," he chuckled. "Your life is surely going to change now."

"No kidding," I said. "Not only do I gain a wife, but I also inherit Sam."

"How old is he?"

"He just turned six. It's been tough for Colleen these last four years, raising him alone and the four years before that putting up with an abusive alcoholic."

"This time," Uncle Bill said, "her luck sure has changed for the better."

"He's a good kid—Sam is—and I have a lot of fun with him. He sure loves it when I get the company hockey tickets and take him to see the Senators."

"They've got a good team this year and could go all the way—if they can get by Hartford."

175

"Yup," I said, "they sure wiped the Canadiens on Friday night."

"Ah, yes," said Uncle Bill. "The once mighty Habitants aren't what they used to be." Suddenly Uncle Bill's face clouded. "You're not here tonight because you're having second thoughts about Colleen, are you?"

"Oh, heck no, Uncle Bill. I couldn't be happier. We're planning the wedding for Labour Day just after the busy season is over and we're going to go down to Barbados for two weeks. Colleen's parents are going to look after Sam the first week and, would you believe, Mom and Dad have volunteered for week two!"

"No kidding," Uncle Bill laughed. "Instant grandparents. How about that? So what's on your mind?"

"A whole bunch of things. Starting with the house."

"What about it?"

"Well, actually, I've been thinking of selling. It's turned out to be a fabulous investment and I've done even better than the projections we worked out five years ago."

"Oh?"

"Yup," I said proudly. "My mortgage stands at only $55,000 instead of the $70,000 that you'd budgeted for after five years."

"So you've paid off an extra $15,000? How'd you do it?"

"Well, first of all, my branch has been doing really well and my income's gone up quite a bit."

"I never realized there was that much money to be made selling knives," mulled Uncle Bill.

"These are real quality. Not only are they better than the Shickels, their leading German-made competitor, but since the new 'Buy North American' campaign took hold two years ago, demand has gone up substantially. These knives are made in Massachusetts and there's talk of setting up a Canadian plant in Arnprior."

Uncle Bill lifted his beer bag in a mock toast.

"Thank goodness for Prime Minister Cormack and President Eastwood. Our government's finally got the brains to realize globalization was killing the North American economy and that we had to bring jobs back to this country, and they finally figured out a way to do it."

176

"Yes," I said. "It was the best publicity campaign that's ever been launched. They simply got everybody onto a 'Buy North American' kick. It's amazing, but it's almost dangerous now to drive a Japanese car. Did you read about those people in Winnipeg who destroyed their neighbour's foreign-made microwave and TV?"

Uncle Bill nodded. "Wanton destruction of property is perhaps a little too much, but if this 'Buy North American' fervour continues, we're likely to see some real advances."

"Unemployment is down to nine per cent," I added.

"Not bad, compared to 14 per cent three years ago. They may eventually get around to balancing their budgets. Who knows? So," he continued, "the knife business has been going great for you. That's terrific!"

"Also," I said nodding, "I never did entirely give up on selling when I got the management position. I convinced the company it would be good for me to keep in contact with customers. That way, I would keep my competitive edge and besides, I'd be able to test all the new marketing techniques as the brain-trust in head office developed them. Also, the territory is large enough that I wasn't taking anything away from my own people."

"So you kept on selling."

"Yes," I said, "basically, two afternoons and one evening a week. And it panned out. I guess I must've earned an average of an extra $10,000 a year in selling commissions alone. It also turned out to be great for staff morale. If I could produce that kind of money on a part-time basis, look how much *they* could earn working at it full-time. And the more they earned, the bigger my override." I rubbed my hands together with glee.

"So, you're laughing all the way to the bank?" asked Uncle Bill.

"That I am," I said with a smile. Suddenly I stared at my uncle as a thought popped into my head. "Uncle Bill, tell me the truth," I asked, "are you disappointed in me?"

"Why should I be disappointed in you?"

"Well, I'm not a professional like Andrea and, at this point anyway, I don't have any great desire to own my own business.

177

Are you disappointed that I'm not more entrepreneurial?"

"Why should I be disappointed? You're happy with what you're doing. Not everybody has to own their own business. You've made an intelligent lifestyle choice. You're doing what I thought you should do all along and that's *working smart, not hard*. You may go out selling one night a week, but you're not working every night and every weekend and you do allow yourself time for holidays. You also seem to be doing pretty well financially for a lad of 26. For that matter, you're doing pretty darn well financially compared to *anybody*, let alone someone your age. There is one thing, though, that I should talk to you about before I forget and then you can tell me what's on *your* mind."

"What's that, Uncle Bill?"

"What do you know about Registered Retirement Savings Plans?"

"Ah ha, I'm way ahead of you. Andrea told me all about them two years ago. She faithfully recounted everything you discussed the weekend of her graduation. I'm in a 45 per cent tax bracket and I've been putting money away in RRSPs each month for the last two years. I'm not up to 18 per cent of my earnings because I've also been making extra payments on my mortgage, but I'm still putting in the same $3,000 a year that she's been contributing. $3,000,000 by age 65 looks pretty good to me and, to tell the truth, I don't miss it. In fact, when the tax refund comes in each year, I take the cheque down to my bank and put it down directly against the mortgage."

"Good plan," said Uncle Bill approvingly. "It won't be long before you don't need my advice any more."

"Oh, I don't think that day is imminent," I said. "In fact, there are a couple of things I did want to talk to you about right now... Getting back to the house."

"Oh yes," said Uncle Bill. "You've got your mortgage down to $55,000. What's the house worth? You paid $104,000, if my memory serves me right."

I nodded. "I had a realtor over and he suggested I list it for $130,000. He figured I'd probably get between $125,000 and $128,000."

"It's a pretty good market and I wouldn't be surprised if he's right," said Uncle Bill. "So, if you got $125,000 net of commission and your mortgage is $55,000, you've got an equity of $70,000 in the property."

"And I figured I'd use that $70,000 towards a new house. There's nothing wrong with the one I'm in, but I bought it at the time with the idea of being close to work and, unfortunately, there really aren't any good parks or bike-riding areas nearby. And now with Sam..."

"I get the picture," said Uncle Bill. "You want something a bit more suburban."

"That's right," I nodded. "Colleen and I found this great house. It's not too big but it's perfect for the three of us and it's right across the street from a park and a bike path. It's listed at $210,000 but it's a divorce situation and the owners are really eager to sell. My realtor figures that we could pick it up for $200,000."

"Has Colleen got any money?"

"Afraid not, Uncle Bill, although she does have some pretty nice furniture. Between the two of us, we should be able to furnish the house in fine style. The artwork she's got isn't expensive but it sure is beautiful. I've never met anybody who's got such a fantastic sense of colour and design. She's also pretty handy with paint and wallpaper. By the time we're finished, it'll be a palace."

"I don't think you should sell your present house," said Uncle Bill.

"But I just explained, I want to move."

"I didn't say you shouldn't move. Your reasons are quite valid. But I don't think you should sell."

"Uncle Bill, you're talking in riddles."

"Okay," he said, "I suppose you're right. What I'm suggesting is *you keep your present house as a rental property and you remortgage it, using the money you borrow as your downpayment for the new house.*"

"Interesting," I said. "My mortgage is actually coming up for renewal on May 10th."

"Here's how I figure it," said Uncle Bill. "You've got an equity of $70,000 in your present house. You can remortgage and borrow about 70 per cent of that or $50,000 out of that equity. In other words, you can renew your mortgage on your property for a total of $105,000—$55,000 to replace what you still owe and $50,000 to take out some of your equity."

"And then if I rent out the upstairs where I've been living for the last five years..." Uncle Bill nodded excitedly as I continued, "the rent I get for the upstairs and the basement will more or less carry the mortgage. Uncle Bill, you're a genius! Sure," I babbled on, thinking out loud, "with the high cost of gasoline, rents in the downtown area have skyrocketed. It might only cost me about $100 a month to carry the house if my tenants pay all the utilities and stuff."

"That's right," said Uncle Bill. "And if there's a short-fall, remember your rental loss can be claimed for income tax."

"You mean if I own rental property and the expenses are bigger than the income, I can claim the loss?"

"In the same way as your RRSP deduction, although you can't make the loss bigger by writing off depreciation."

"So by allowing these deductions the government subsidizes the ownership of rental property?"

"Exactly," said Uncle Bill. "If you're in a 45 per cent tax-bracket and your mortgage interest, taxes and so on exceed your rental income by, say, $2,000 over the course of the year, when the smoke clears it'll only cost you $1,100."

"So I can take $50,000 out of my refinancing money and use *that* towards the downpayment on a new house."

"As long as you can afford the mortgage payments."

"I'm pretty sure I can, Uncle Bill. I've budgeted $2,600 a month for the house and $150,000 at eight per cent will only cost $2,110 a month."

"How long is your amortization?" asked Uncle Bill sternly.

"A full payout over eight years, of course," I said proudly.

"Good man," my uncle said. "By your age 35, you'll have that house paid for. One way to arrange your financing is to set up, say, a 20-year payment plan, but to make additional payments along the way that will reduce the payout to only eight years. If times get rough, you would have the option of forgoing the extra payments for a period of time. This is a good safety net. You'd then be able to catch up later when you're able. Remember the benefits of making your mortgage payments bi-weekly instead of only once a month."

"You've taught me well," I complimented him. "If there's one thing I now understand, it's the advantage of mortgage acceleration payments."

"But what about taxes and utilities?"

"Well, to be honest, Colleen and I figure it'll cost about $700 or $800 a month."

"So you're a bit short?"

"It's not that serious, though, because Sam will be going to school full-time starting in September and Colleen plans to work three days a week as a receptionist with an interior designer. The lady who presently has the job just found out she's pregnant and she's going on maternity leave in September. The timing couldn't be better. Also, Colleen is taking courses in home design using virtual reality technology. We both think that's a great career for her because she'll have flexible hours and I'm looking forward to volunteering our new house for her to practice on."

"I'll bet you are," said Uncle Bill with a smile.

"Well, I sure am glad I came here tonight. What a fabulous idea, to keep my house and still be able to trade up to a new one! I guess I've got my financial picture well in hand for now, thanks to you."

"Not so fast," said Uncle Bill, "there are still a couple of things you've never had to think about before that are suddenly important."

"Really?" I said. "I thought I had it all covered."

"Nope," said Uncle Bill. "Now that you're going to be a married man with an instant family, you've got to think about life insurance and making a will."

❦

Without waiting for my response, Uncle Bill stood up and walked into his kitchen, returning a moment later with two steaming cups of coffee. I took the time to allow my thoughts to focus on this new uncharted territory.

"Life insurance? Is that a major problem?" I asked as he sat down.

"Not really," replied Uncle Bill. "Fortunately you're very young and the cost isn't that expensive at your age. Life insurance is a bet. You bet you're going to die and the insurance company bets you're going to live. Fortunately, the odds are on their side. So for a few dollars a month, you can buy quite a bit of coverage. Consider this," he continued. "If you were to drop dead today, what would you want Colleen to have?"

"Well," I thought for a moment, "it would be nice if she had the house paid for. In fact, if she had *both* properties paid for, she could live in our new house and earn the rental income on the other one without having to pay out anything to a mortgage company. That alone would give her an income of about $1,100 a month and no rent payment of her own to worry about."

"So you'd need $250,000 of coverage just for your mortgages. That's about right. What else?"

"I guess another $250,000 so she could live off the interest."

"And?"

"And another $100,000 to cover Sam's expenses until he's all grown up and through with his education."

"Good," said Uncle Bill.

"That's about $600,000 in total."

"Actually, it wouldn't hurt for you to have an extra $150,000 over and above for total insurance coverage of $750,000. Until Colleen finishes her design course, it doesn't sound like she can earn a lot of money. So you may as well protect her and I think you'll find the additional premiums aren't too heavy."

"$750,000." I whistled. "That's a lot of insurance."

"But it's necessary and at least it's after-tax money."

"What do you mean by after-tax money when you're talking about life insurance?"

"Under Canadian tax law, life insurance premiums are usually not allowed as a tax deduction," Uncle Bill said. "There is an exception in certain business situations but that doesn't apply in your case. On the other hand, when an insured person dies, the proceeds are paid to the beneficiary tax-free. So whatever you, uh, I mean your estate receives from the insurance company is free and clear."

"Great, we have to wait until we're dead to get a tax break," I muttered. "Isn't that typical?" I had never heard my Uncle Bill roar with laughter before but it happened just then. I began to suspect that besides being a math and investment whiz, my uncle had a weird sense of humour.

"For someone who hasn't given life insurance any thought at all before, your analysis isn't bad," he said as he got control of his laughter. "Now, what if Colleen died?" he asked. "What would she want you to have?"

"Well, if I only had my one income coming in and I was going to look after Sam—which I would want to do—it would be nice if the house were paid for. But I wouldn't need much more as long as I'm able to work."

"A noble sentiment," said Uncle Bill, "but not necessarily sensible. Besides, what's good for the goose is good for the gander. I'm sure if you asked Colleen, she would say she would like you to have some money if anything happened to her. You'd probably need more than you think because you'd probably want a housekeeper to help you look after Sam." He paused then to pick up his reading glasses and wipe them and I could envision the cogs and gears working in his head. The glasses thing was a trick, to give him time to collect his thoughts. He must've been a heck of a teacher, probably one of the few people who could make income taxes anything other than boring.

"I think if you were covered for $750,000 and Colleen for $500,000, you'd be in pretty good shape. You could always reassess your situation every few years."

"You wouldn't happen to know how expensive it would be if Colleen and I had this coverage?" I wondered.

"They don't publish insurance rates, Logan, so I can't just pull out a book and give you a figure," Uncle Bill replied. "But I don't think it's nearly as expensive as you would think. With your needs and financial situation, the two of you don't require anything more than pure term insurance. And I'll bet you could get everything you need for about $1,000 a year. You're both in good shape. I assume that Colleen is, like yourself, a non-smoker."

I nodded.

"Term insurance is relatively cheap," Uncle Bill continued.

"Term insurance?" I shook my head. "I'm sorry to be so ignorant Uncle Bill, but what is term insurance?"

"Don't apologize, Logan. If we were all to apologize for everything we didn't know, the world would come to a standstill, with everyone apologizing to everyone else all day long every day of their lives."

"You're right," I conceded. "I guess I have no reason to apologize for not knowing something I never needed to know before."

"Good," Uncle Bill nodded. "Now, in simple language, term insurance is a straight bet between the insurance company and the insured. As I said before, the insured bets he or she will die and the insurance company bets he or she will live. So, for a one-year term insurance policy at your age, you'd likely pay about $600 to entice a particular company to bet with you. They're willing to bet your few hundred against their $750,000. The reason is, maybe only one in a thousand 26 year olds dies and most of those who do aren't insurable in the first place. So it's a good bet from the insurance company's perspective."

"But if I'm not going to die, why do I need the insurance?"

"Well you never know, *some* people die. You could be hit by a truck for example, or suffer a sudden illness. It isn't likely you would be the one in a thousand to suddenly keel over but it could happen and you don't want to take the gamble of leaving Colleen without a decent financial buffer. Since you've put together an eight-year plan to pay off your mortgage, I suggest you and Colleen each take out 10-year term insurance policies for $750,000 and $500,000 respectively, with each of you as the other's beneficiary. By the end of the 10 years, your houses will be paid and you should have some fairly substantial RRSP savings."

"I imagine I can get it from any insurance company or agent. Piece of cake."

"Except you want to shop around."

"Huh?" I grunted. "Shop around for what?"

"The best rates you can get," Uncle Bill said. "The insurance business is pretty competitive and every insurer offers a range of products. Actually, it can get pretty confusing and complicated."

I groaned. "It looks like I'm going to have to become an accountant like you after all."

"No, my boy, technology is your friend here. Specifically, computers. There's a company right here in Ontario called Compulife that provides a computerized price quotation service for insurance brokers and agents with monthly information updates. All the agent or broker has to do is type in your particulars: male, 26, non-smoker, and the desired coverage, in your case $750,000 for 10-year term insurance. Then the computer spits out as many as 50 different quotations from various insurance companies."

"Finally, something that's going to take less than a lifetime to deal with," I smiled.

"Yes, my boy. Computers are wondrous things," Uncle Bill beamed. "Now, you'll want the opportunity to renew your 10-year policy at the end of the 10 years without proving your health is good. It'll cost a bit extra to get this option but it's worthwhile. Again, the product I suggest for you and Colleen is 10-year renewable term."

"10-year renewable term," I said under my breath as I pulled out a pencil and a sliver of paper and wrote it down.

"I think we've pinpointed enough details that this Compulife thing should work for you. A friend of mine in Hull who sells insurance showed me how it works and it's a dream." Uncle Bill cocked his head to one side. "Though you might not necessarily pick the company that quotes the cheapest premium. Fortunately, some companies offer special rates for persons who have never smoked and you and Colleen would both qualify."

"Actually," I interrupted, "Colleen used to smoke until she got pregnant with Sam."

"Well," Uncle Bill continued, "at least you'd qualify then. Some insurers are tiny operations and you might not want to take the risk of dealing with a company you've not heard of, but you'll hit names you'll recognize and you'll find, depending on circumstances, London Life might be a better bet for you than Financial Life. On the other hand, Financial Life might come out ahead of London Life for Colleen."

"Well, at least we're both in good health even though Colleen is four months older than I am. Did I tell you she's planning to run a marathon this summer?"

Uncle Bill shook his head and continued his life insurance lecture. "You never know what you'll find. As I understand it, the various insurance companies try to balance their risks and actually have sales—just like department stores. For example, a particular company at a given point in time might be trying to entice smokers between ages 50 and 55."

Uncle Bill held up his hand to keep me from interrupting with the all-too-obvious question. "Odd, I know, selling to higher-risk individuals, except they figure they can balance their portfolio and earn a good premium for the risk. That same company eager to attract this particular market might not want to offer great deals for males between ages 25 and 30. So there's no way to know, at any given time, which company is the best one unless you check."

"So where do I get my hands on this program?" I asked.

"You don't," replied Uncle Bill. "You just find an insurance broker or agent who uses the Compulife program and is willing to back up his or her recommendation with hard data on what different companies are charging. If you want, I can phone around and see if I can find someone to help you."

"No, thanks, Uncle Bill. Actually, Colleen has an aunt who owns her own insurance brokerage business. I'll call her on Monday for some quotes."

❧

Uncle Bill was right. We were able to get what we needed for about $1,000 a year. I spoke to Colleen later that evening and she called her aunt, Marlene Devlin, the one who owns her own insurance agency. We were able to get in to see her the next afternoon. Marlene said her agency was one of hundreds of independent agencies across the country who subscribe to

Compulife and she was impressed we knew about the service. She agreed that 10-year renewable term was the way for us to go. I still have the papers she produced to back up her recommendations. I chose Standard Life Assurance at an annual cost of $665, and Colleen's policy cost $340 from Westbury Canadian. We didn't go with the cheapest because Marlene suggested we factor in the annual renewal cost after 10 years. On balance, we chose what we liked best looking at the next 20 years in total. It was interesting to see how different companies were ahead of others in different situations and how the rates varied dramatically from company to company. When I saw how Standard's coverage would only cost me $665, while many others would charge well over $800 for the same coverage, I realized how important it is to shop the market for insurance...for almost anything.

Colleen and I arranged to pay the premiums monthly as an automatic charge against our joint bank account. I must admit, though, I resented paying for something I never wanted either of us to collect. But, as I took a step back and examined our situation, I could see how important adequate protection was, and is. Looking back over the years, I suppose Colleen and I laid out a great deal of money we might have better used in other areas. But at least we're alive and well, and when I look at the obituaries in any newspaper and see how many people do, in fact, die young, in their prime years, it becomes evident that life insurance is an important component of anyone's financial planning, especially if they have dependents. (As I get older, I find I sound more and more like Uncle Bill. You know something...I like it. There are worse models I could've picked.)

❧

"Well," I said to Uncle Bill. "We've accomplished enough for one night, what with all this deep discussion about housing and life insurance. What do you say we catch the last half of the Senators' game? They're playing in Saskatoon tonight." I started to reach for Uncle Bill's remote.

"Not so fast," he said. "There's still one more thing. We should talk about your will." He paused a moment and looked closely at me. "You do have a will, don't you?" he asked slowly.

I hung my head in reply while Uncle Bill shook his head stoically.

"Well I suppose up 'til now it wasn't all that important, although once a person starts to build up some assets, it's always a good idea to prepare a will. But now that you're getting married...your first order of business is to see a lawyer immediately, like tomorrow, and prepare a will. It won't cost you much money because your situation is pretty straightforward. I imagine you'll want to leave your property to Colleen."

I nodded in agreement.

"You can disagree with me if you want," Uncle Bill continued, "but as I see it, the proper way for most people to make a will is simply to leave all assets to a spouse—preferably their own." He chuckled. "The tax rules in Canada actually encourage this approach because all the property can pass from husband to wife or wife to husband tax-free. This includes things like real estate, RRSPs and mutual fund investments and so on. It's only when the second spouse dies that Canadian capital gains provisions kick in if there is property outside of a principal residence that has appreciated in value."

I — BEING OF SOUND MIND, HAVE DECIDED TO TAKE IT WITH ME

"How does the RRSP work, again, Uncle Bill?"

"If you leave your RRSP to Colleen and she leaves hers to you, once she has one, there are no taxes when

188

the first of you dies. The survivor gets to put the deceased's RRSP into his or her own plan and draw the income from it as would have been the case before."

"So, what you're saying then is that in most cases, it's perfectly acceptable for husbands to leave their estates to their wives and vice versa."

"Who else would a spouse worry about?" Uncle Bill asked.

I shrugged.

"Well, there are exceptions," Uncle Bill volunteered. "For example, if you're very wealthy and you have grown-up children, you might want to leave some property directly to them. There are also some complex situations such as when there is a marriage later in life and both parties have children by previous marriages. A person might want to leave the bulk of an estate to his or her own kids and not necessarily to the spouse's kids. But your situation is pretty straightforward and there's no need to make something overly complicated when it's simple. In a nutshell, you and Colleen need wills."

"Colleen, too?"

"Well, once she has her life insurance policy, even if there's nothing else, she'll have a substantial estate as well. She might want to leave part of her estate to Sam with you as trustee. If I were her, I'd leave, say, half the insurance to you so you could pay off the house, and the remainder I'd have you hold in trust for Sam's support and education. Do you have a lawyer or would you like me to recommend one?"

"Actually, we should be okay on that as well, Uncle Bill. Colleen's Aunt Marlene's husband, Tom, is a lawyer. In fact, Tom and Marlene share offices together, so we'll be able to kill two birds with one stone. Since my situation is simpler than Colleen's, I think I'll suggest she might want to meet with Tom first and talk with him alone. After all, she has to be assured that Sam's welfare will be looked after. Anyway, I can assure you, we'll get right on top of it."

"Good," said Uncle Bill. "Now, what are you waiting for? That hockey game must be more than half over."

189

COMPULIFE SOFTWARE INC.

Term Survey—10 Year Renewable

Face Amount: $750,000

Proposal for Logan Lavery   Prepared by Marlene Devlin

Age Last Birthday: 26 Age Nearest Birthday: 26 Male Non-smoker

---

INDUSTRIAL-ALLIANCE LIFE INSURANCE
10 YEAR RENEWABLE & CONVERTIBLE TERM

	PROJECTED	GUARANTEED
Age 26		652.50
Age 36	1,012.50*	1,522.50
Age 46	2,310.00*	3,465.00
Age 56	5,775.00*	8,662.50
Age 66	15,225.00*	22,837.50

RENEWABLE TO 70 CONVERTIBLE TO 65

NORTH WEST LIFE ASSURANCE COMPANY
TERM 10 –10 YEAR R & C TERM

	PROJECTED	GUARANTEED
Age26		652.50
Age 36	1,012.50*	1,522.50
Age 46	2,310.00*	3,465.00
Age 56	5,775.00	*8,662.50
Age 66	15,225.00*	22,837.50

RENEWABLE TO 70 CONVERTIBLE TO 65

THE STANDARD LIFE ASSURANCE COMPANY
10 YEAR RENEWABLE & CONVERTIBLE TERM

	GUARANTEED
Age 26	665.00
Age 36	972.50
Age 46	2,330.00
Age 56	5,585.00
Age 66	15,027.50
Age 76	39,545.00

RENEWABLE TO 80 CONVERTIBLE TO 65

TRANSAMERICA LIFE INSURANCE COMPANY
10 YEAR CONVERTIBLE AND RENEWABLE

	GUARANTEED
Age 26	680.00
Age 36	1,347.50
Age 46	2,720.00
Age 56	6,935.00
Age 66	18,732.50
Age 76	40,377.50

RENEWABLE TO 80 CONVERTIBLE TO 71

AMERICAN LIFE INSURANCE COMPANY
TERM PLUS –10 YEAR R & C TERM

	GUARANTEED
Age 26	685.00
Age 36	1,015.00
Age 46	2,170.00
Age 56	5,290.00
Age 66	13,480.00

ORIGINAL AGE ENHANCEMENT (RATE) OPTION
RENEWABLE TO 75 CONVERTIBLE TO 65

THE EMPIRE LIFE INSURANCE COMPANY
TERM 10/10

	GUARANTEED
Age 26	710.00
Age 36	1,175.00

RENEWABLE TO 46 CONVERTIBLE TO 36

LEGEND: * VALUE PROJECTED, NOT GUARANTEED

NOTE: EVERY EFFORT HAS BEEN MADE TO ASSURE THE ACCURACY OF THIS INFORMATION BUT WE CANNOT GUARANTEE ACCURACY AND ARE NOT LIABLE FOR ERRORS OR OMISSIONS

COMPULIFE SOFTWARE INC.

Term Survey—10 Year Renewable

Face Amount: $500,000

Proposal for Colleen Lavery   Prepared by Marlene Devlin

Age Last Birthday: 26   Age Nearest Birthday: 26   Female Non-smoker

---

FINANCIAL LIFE ASSURANCE COMPANY

CHOICE TERM 10

	GUARANTEED
Age 26	330.00
Age 36	750.00
Age 41	1,145.00
Age 46	1,645.00
Age 51	2,190.00
Age 56	3,140.00

RENEWABLE TO 80 CONVERTIBLE TO 65

WESTBURY CANADIAN LIFE INSURANCE COMPANY

TERM 10 –10 YEAR R & C TERM

	GUARANTEED
Age 26	340.00
Age 36	650.00
Age 46	1,245.00
Age 56	3,060.00
Age 66	7,540.00
Age 76	25,270.00

GIC OPTION INCLUDED FOR AGES UP TO 55
RENEWABLE TO 80 CONVERTIBLE TO 70

INDUSTRIAL-ALLIANCE LIFE INSURANCE

10 YEAR RENEWABLE & CONVERTIBLE TERM

	PROJECTED	GUARANTEED
Age 26		345.00
Age 36	535.00*	805.00
Age 46	1,225.00*	1,840.00
Age 56	2,550.00*	3,825.00
Age 66	6,185.00*	9,280.00

RENEWABLE TO 70 CONVERTIBLE TO 65

THE NORTH WEST LIFE ASSURANCE COMPANY

TERM 10 –10 YEAR R & C TERM

	PROJECTED	GUARANTEED
Age 26		345.00
Age 36	535.00*	805.00
Age 46	1,225.00*	1,840.00
Age 56	2,550.00*	3,825.00
Age 66	6,185.00*	9,280.00

RENEWABLE TO 70 CONVERTIBLE TO 65

ZURICH LIFE INSURANCE COMPANY OF CANADA

10 YEAR RENEWABLE & CONVERTIBLE TERM

	GUARANTEED
Age 26	345.00
Age 36	645.00
Age 46	1,505.00
Age 56	2,560.00
Age 66	5,835.00
Age 76	20,145.00

RENEWABLE TO 80 CONVERTIBLE TO 70

TRANSAMERICA LIFE INSURANCE COMPANY

10 YEAR CONVERTIBLE AND RENEWABLE

	GUARANTEED
Age 26	355.00
Age 36	745.00
Age 46	1,500.00
Age 56	3,630.00
Age 66	8,940.00
Age 76	20,510.00

RENEWABLE TO 80 CONVERTIBLE TO 71

LEGEND: * VALUE PROJECTED, NOT GUARANTEED
NOTE: EVERY EFFORT HAS BEEN MADE TO ASSURE THE ACCURACY OF THIS INFORMATION BUT WE CANNOT GUARANTEE ACCURACY AND ARE NOT LIABLE FOR ERRORS OR OMISSIONS

ANDREA'S STORY:
TAKING CARE OF BUSINESS

"COME ON IN," Uncle Bill called as his front door was opened by one of those new computer-controlled voice-activated servo-motor systems.

"It's good to see you, my dear," Uncle Bill said as I walked into his apartment, kicked off my shoes, and padded gratefully over to his living room couch. I had had another run-in with head office that afternoon and was feeling quite out of sorts. They kept trying to insist I reduce the time for a standard eye examination in the interests of squeezing in an extra two patients into each eight-hour day. I've always been a great believer in efficiency, but there has to be a limit. I hoped I would always put patient care ahead of the almighty dollar.

"Would you like a coffee?" asked Uncle Bill. "Nora's playing bridge tonight and we're on our own."

"Just what the doctor ordered," I answered.

"Regular, Swiss Chocolate or Raspberry Rhubarb?" he asked. "I've got this newfangled coffee-maker that lets me choose from up to three blends. It brews two mugs in less than a minute and it's as good as anything you get in a restaurant. Best of all, this little darling was invented right here in Canada, and it's manufactured in Winnipeg."

"How about the coffee?" I asked. "Locally grown as well?"

"Hydroponically in Whitehorse, as a matter of fact," Uncle Bill said proudly. "I defy you to tell the difference between this blend and the old South American stuff."

"And probably a tenth of the price," I muttered.

"The price of somebody's misbegotten idea of progress,"

Uncle Bill said. "The World Bank finances South American oil exploration and cattle ranching. The explorers devastate the crop lands. The ranchers turn it into grazing. Both cut down the rainforests and the erosion destroys more land." He shook his head in frustration.

"Well, at least the World Bank has learned its lesson or the bad press hit it hard," I said.

"Whatever the case, a few days ago, the World Bank put up the last $10,000,000 for the new Ndoki World Heritage Rainforest Preserve in the Northern Congo." Uncle Bill snorted. "So sponsoring a few hundred miles of rainforest is all it takes to redeem oneself for raping the land?"

I shrugged. "Better than nothing and we end up picking up the slack in Arctic Canada by recycling residual heat from industrial and municipal operations for use in agriculture, specialty items, cash crops and so on."

We both fell silent. Both of our worlds weren't even adequate that day. Two minutes later, I was adding my standard half-teaspoon of sugar and a bit of milk to my cup of Raspberry Rhubarb. Uncle Bill took his black, the better to savour the taste. I settled back into the comfort of the couch, sipped the coffee and sighed.

"So, what's on your mind?" Uncle Bill asked. "You look like you're carrying the weight of the world on your shoulders."

"Maybe not the weight of the world, Uncle Bill, but I think the time has come for me to go out on my own. We run a pretty good practice over at Cyclops but the overhead is killing us. They lose a fortune each year on shoplifting and breakage in their stores and they expect us to pick up the slack. The pressure is on to see too darn many patients each day and I don't like to do sloppy work. I think the time has finally come for me to open up my own shop. But I'm scared. What if I don't make it?"

"Have you considered going into practice with some of your colleagues?"

"I've looked into a couple of situations, but unfortunately I'd be low person on the totem pole and I'm kind of tired of office politics. It also seems they all want a heck of a lot of money for goodwill to let a new person in."

"So what's wrong with starting your own shop or buying a business outright?"

"I'm not sure I can handle it, Uncle Bill."

"Sure you can," he said. "Starting up or buying a new business isn't necessarily as hard as one might think—if you know what you're doing—and you've had over five years' experience. Why don't we see what's available? Do you want to stay here in Ottawa?"

"It's my home," I said. "I've got my family here, my friends; I wouldn't want to move unless I had to."

"Okay, come with me. I want to show you something." Uncle Bill led me into the spare bedroom he used as an office. We sat down in front of a computer terminal and he flipped a switch.

"Good evening, Bill," the computer said. "What can I do for you today?"

The voice sounded like Kathleen Turner's, Uncle Bill's favourite old-time movie actress—amazingly soft, throaty and sexy.

"Good evening, Catherine," he replied. "Please search the Ottawa Public Database for Ottawa Times-Herald Business-to-Business Section for the week to date." The terminal lit up and faded to the scene on Uncle Bill's Thinitron that evening—a Nova Scotia harbour scene with soft, rolling fog whispering around small fishing boats bobbing on the water. Then the machine hummed at us. I mean it actually hummed at us. For all that he had been an accountant, Uncle Bill has a curiosity about and love for technology that was rare in people of his age and era. He was always buying new gadgets to try them out, though he never abandoned that little pocket calculator of his. Some day, when he's gone, I'd like to get it as a memento of him, although I'll probably have to fight Logan for it. That evening, his computer hummed a little tune at us, the way a person would, you know...absent-mindedly while working on something. Shortly, the harbour scene faded, text scrolled across the screen telling us we were in and that same sweet voice emanated from the computer.

"Please describe your business parameters, Bill."

"Small optometry practice."

"With eyeglass and contact lens dispensary," I reminded him.

"With eyeglass and contact lens dispensary, within a 50-mile radius of Ottawa."

"There are three listings," the computer replied. "Do you have any further specifications?"

"Investment capital required $200,000 or less, Catherine. Required rate of return on investment capital, a minimum of 20 per cent. The opportunity to earn between $60,000 and $100,000 a year from the owner's own efforts." The machine blinked. I swear it did—or something like that, then spoke.

"There are two listings that meet these parameters. Would you like a printed list, Bill?"

"Yes, thank you, Catherine," Uncle Bill said. The red light on the printer lit up and the list dropped to the paper tray.

"Can you believe how much computers have changed?" Uncle Bill asked. "I find myself saying please and thank you as if I were talking to a human being. But then again, this computer is smarter than most people I know, present company excepted, of course."

"Of course," I agreed. "You should leave your estate to your computer so it can buy its own electricity and components."

"I'll consider it, along with leaving a fortune to stray cats and honest politicians," Uncle Bill said with a crooked grin. "Now let's talk about starting or buying a new business. Maybe I can alleviate some of your fears. Let's go back to the living room."

We took our coffee mugs and settled back on the couch. I turned my attention to the Maritime harbour scene. Uncle Bill touched a switch on a small console next to his chair and the lights dimmed. A soft fog started to enter the room through the vents. I could hear the soft lapping of waves on the shore and, in the distance, the muted sound of a foghorn.

"The way I see it," said Uncle Bill, "there are four criteria for business success and although you don't exactly meet all four criteria head on, the fact that you know what you're doing should work in your favour. Besides, I've never known an optometrist who starved to death."

"I knew it," I smiled in triumph. "You've set the stage here for another lecture. Four criteria indeed. I'll bite... what might they be, Uncle Bill?" I asked sweetly in
my best child's voice.

"I've believed for years there are four criteria a person should consider before starting or buying a business," he said, dropping into his professorial style. "In no particular order they are—," he ticked them off on his fingers as he spoke, "*one*, you don't want a business in which you have to maintain a significant inventory, especially any inventory subject to obsolescence; *two*, you don't want a business that is capital intensive and requires a significant investment in machinery and equipment; *three*, the product or service you furnish should be, if at all possible, recession-proof; and *four*, in general, you should provide products, not personal services, to your customers."

"Nice list," I said. "Could you go through them one-by-one with some more detail?"

"Did you think I would do otherwise?" Uncle Bill asked, his eyes a-twinkle. He didn't wait for an answer. "I've got all evening and so do you. Another coffee?"

"No, thanks. But did you remember to turn off your computer before we went back into the living room? I wouldn't want Catherine giving away your trade secrets to anybody else."

"Don't worry," said Uncle Bill. "Catherine can be trusted. Her loyalty is beyond reproach." Uncle Bill fiddled with his remote control unit and a small campfire suddenly materialized on the sandy beach by the seashore. The crackling of the burning wood contrasted sharply with the soft movement of the waves and the distant foghorn.

"First, some background," he finally said, as he adjusted the scene from dusk, through twilight, to evening. "The biggest problem that has always faced new business operators is under-capitalization. Many people have had good ideas over the years but they haven't had enough money to carry through. Fortunately, since 2002, we now have a Small Business Financing Act in place and the banks are willing to lend money if they think there's a decent chance of success. In your case, as a professional, you should be able to get financing."

"I've got over $50,000 in RRSPs," I said proudly.

"You've got a good track record," Uncle Bill smiled. "You've got a profession and no bad history with credit cards. I'm sure they'll take a risk on you. Now, remember my first criterion: you don't want to have a business that has to carry a significant amount of inventory because your financing costs can kill you if your inventory doesn't turn over fast enough. Part of the problem is that inventory purchases are usually covered with borrowed money. And with floating interest rates, businesses can't effectively budget for interest costs because they never know what they'll actually be. Unfortunately, most politicians are lawyers, not businessmen, and what they don't realize is that this country needs a stable interest policy where the rates are *not* allowed to fluctuate each week. God knows how many letters I've written to the Prime Minister, the Finance Minister and various senior cabinet people, but they won't listen."

"You couldn't have chosen an easier issue to fight over?" I asked.

"No," Uncle Bill growled. "Unless business owners can count on a stable interest rate for anywhere from two to five years, it's almost impossible for them to budget for the cost of borrowed money. Let's assume a business borrows $100,000. If the interest rate over a five-year period averages seven per cent, the total cost over that time is $35,000. If the average interest rate is 12 per cent, the interest becomes $60,000, almost double. That $25,000 spread could be the difference between being profitable and going broke. You can budget for rent, you can budget for salaries, you can set a limit for advertising and promotion, but the one area that small business has no control over is financing costs."

I had never seen Uncle Bill get so agitated over an issue or idea. Mind you, we had never talked about interest except as something that is an ally in establishing security. This was a whole new side of interest—something I would need to pay attention to because, as scary as the idea of going into business sounded to me, I was starting to like it.

I rejoined Uncle Bill in mid-rant—"even if this means our dollar falls relative to the U.S. dollar or other currencies, we need a stable interest rate," he grumbled. "Until we have interest rate stability my first criterion stands. You don't want a business in which you must tie up a lot of money, especially borrowed money, in inventory. In your case, fortunately, you'll probably be able to order lenses, frames, and so on from the manufacturers as you need them, so your kind of business should pass the first test."

"Quite easily," I said. "The manufacturers are more than happy to provide us with displays and samples that we put up in our fitting room and when I order, I can get next-day turn around, tops two days. I've already done some figuring and I don't think I need more than about $10,000 for inventory."

"Good, that's one problem solved," Uncle Bill grinned. "Whatever you do, stay away from any business that requires you to carry a lot of inventory. This is especially true if products are seasonal or subject to obsolescence."

"I know what you mean about that," I said. "I once tried to figure out the logic behind a Christmas ornament shop that went broke. The owners had a whopping good selling season in October, November and December. But whatever they didn't sell before Christmas, they had to hold on to for at least eight or nine slow months..."

"I know the store," Uncle Bill said. "The owners were stuck financing an inventory that wasn't moving."

"It's funny, though," I said. "Last winter we took a two-week ski vacation to Banff in your old home province of Alberta. There's a similar shop on the main street that's been in business for 30 years."

"But it's in a tourist location where people buy things just for having been there, so it really isn't just a Christmas decoration store. Think of it as a shop that deals in the novelty of selling Christmas goods to tourists. Remember, business is marketing. Positioning. Positioning. Positioning."

"I see your point how the inventory issue is a big one for anybody starting a business."

Uncle Bill nodded. "I don't think you're too young to remember how so many of the giant retail chains collapsed or were seriously down-sized in the early '90s. Sears gave up its catalogue business, Woodward's in the west was taken over and the name disappeared, Birks Jewellers went bankrupt, then found a buyer who saved the company and so on."

"Those weren't good times in the retail industry," I agreed, "so I have no doubt about your first point. Fortunately, an optometry practice with a dispensary is a business where inventory carrying costs won't kill me. Now, what's the second criterion?"

"You don't want anything that is too heavily capital intensive," Uncle Bill said.

I nodded. "You mean a business where the owner has to buy a lot of machinery and equipment. Sounds a lot like the problem with inventory."

"Exactly," Uncle Bill gleamed. "If you have to spend hundreds of thousands of dollars buying equipment, then again, your carrying costs can kill you. When it comes to equipment, you not only have to pay interest charges but, over a period of time, you have to pay for the capital cost of the equipment as well. At least you can sell inventory at a profit—you hope—and buy more, but with equipment, you generally keep it and it depreciates over time."

"But doesn't the tax system help out by letting people claim depreciation on the equipment which somehow offsets income, Uncle Bill?" I objected. "Even I know that much."

"Yes, but most equipment really does depreciate over time and eventually it has to be replaced. A major investment in machinery and equipment can cripple even big companies and that's something a fledgling entrepreneur should avoid."

"Well, unfortunately, I may have a problem here because, as you might know, an optometry practice requires a fair investment in equipment."

"How much?"

"I've done some checking and there are companies that will provide what they call *a turn-key operation*. They'll install all the equipment I would need and lease it to me with a seven-year payout. The value is about $200,000 and I can pay it off at $3,500 a month."

"Have you calculated the interest rate?"

I blushed in response.

Uncle Bill reached over to the coffee table and picked up the same little calculator he'd brought back from Germany six years earlier.

201

"I see you've still got this little machine," I said.

"Yup, it still works pretty well, although there are some new North American models that are just as good," he said proudly. "Every once in a while, this one over here crosses me up by lapsing into German."

I laughed.

He pressed a couple of buttons. "Amount of loan $200,000, monthly payments $3,500, payout period seven years." He pressed another button. "Input complete. What is the interest rate?"

"Zwolf Prözent," said the computer.

"See what I mean?" said Uncle Bill. "I've had to learn some basic German to work with this thing. Take a guess."

I shrugged my shoulders.

"12 per cent. Instead of paying 12 per cent to a leasing company, you could probably borrow $200,000 at the bank and it would only cost you eight per cent."

"So what would my monthly payments be?"

"I suppose this machine could tell me but it's probably just as quick for me to look it up in Zimmer's 'Money Manager'."

"I see you keep that on your coffee table as well."

"My dear, I am an accountant, you know. And you never know when I'm going to have to look up some numbers. Let's see...at eight per cent interest compounded monthly it takes 0.0156 per month—in other words about a cent and a half to amortize $1 at eight per cent over seven years. That means $200,000 would cost 0.0156 times $200,000 or $3,120."

"That's quite a difference."

"You better believe it," said Uncle Bill. "I'm sure with your track record you can get your bank to finance you. If you had to put up a lot of money for inventory then you might be better off with the leasing option to preserve your line of credit at the bank. But since you don't need a line of credit for inventory, I think the bank will finance your equipment."

"The good news is what I buy will probably last at least ten years before it becomes obsolete, and, fortunately, I don't need a lot of space."

"What do you mean?" It was Uncle Bill's turn to ask me.

"Well, if I had a business with a lot of inventory and a great deal of equipment, I would need a lot more space and that would clearly increase my overhead—rent, utilities, and the like. Low inventory means less space. The equipment is expensive but it doesn't take up a whole lot of room."

"You're thinking like a business person already," Uncle Bill crowed. "See how easy it is?"

I smiled and for the first time in a few days I didn't feel like my face was cracking because I grinned. "So, what's your third criterion, Oh Wise Master?" I bowed slightly. "I'm all ears."

"And damn good that you are," Uncle Bill chuckled. "The next criterion is you want a recession-proof business. One for which people need you whether times are good or bad. Remember the Birks bankruptcy of the early '90s I referred to? Birks wasn't the only jewelry company to hit on hard times."

"Of course not," I said. "Uncle Bill, that was during one of the worst depressions we've had since the end of World War II. People just weren't buying jewelry."

"Exactly," Uncle Bill replied. "No matter how good your product, if people don't consider it necessary in bad times they just aren't going to buy. But you've never heard of a pharmacy chain going bankrupt, have you?"

"No, can't say that I have."

"Why would that be?"

"I guess because people get sick in good *and* bad times, probably more in the bad because of the stress," I suggested. "And things like kleenex and toilet paper are staples and the sales volumes don't vary much whether the economy is up or down."

"See, you know more about business and economics than you give yourself credit for, Andrea," Uncle Bill said. "Mind you, becoming an economic expert probably doesn't require zillions of years of training. Anyone who can think clearly can be an economist."

"Great. Maybe I'll set up an economic consulting division to my business," I suggested brightly.

"Go away," Uncle Bill growled. "Too many amateurs and witch doctors muddying up the field. Stick to what you know best—optometry. Even with the advances in laser surgery, people still need glasses and contact lenses. I don't think you'll ever be obsolete. In one way, you're very lucky. You happened to pick a field that's recession-proof. You're a lot better off than many engineers and architects."

"You're right there, Uncle Bill," I said happily. "And the last criterion?"

"I think the best businesses are those that provide products and not personal services. Now here the idea of an optometry practice doesn't quite fit, but one does have to make compromises."

"You've just confused the issue, Uncle Bill."

"Sorry, Andrea, but let me explain," Uncle Bill said. "If you provide products for resale, you profit from marking up these goods above your cost. Obviously, the mark-up must factor in your *overhead costs*, such as office rent, office supplies and stationery, and so on. The problem with being in a business that provides personal services is you must always work or you aren't earning money."

I groaned.

"Actually, your situation isn't that terrible. You wouldn't be in your office all alone, would you?"

"No, I'd need an optician and a receptionist to start."

"The receptionist is overhead but the optician is going to earn you money. Is that not so?"

"I suppose you're right, Uncle Bill. I expect I'll earn enough profit from the sale of glasses and lenses to cover my optician's salary and then some."

"Good," Uncle Bill nodded. "Now, what happens when you take holidays?"

"I suppose I'd do the same as Dad used to do. He hired a pharmacist to replace himself and the business kept operating. He always complained that profits went down when he and Mom were away. But, come to think of it, he never complained about losing."

"Exactly," said Uncle Bill. "When you go away on holidays, you can hire an optometrist to substitute for you. Even after factoring the salary cost, you should still make some profit."

"I see your point. As long as the business runs smoothly while I'm away I don't even have to make a whole lot of money on the substitute. I'll get my profits from the sale of glasses, contact lenses and so on. I guess my business is really a combination of products and services."

"And what do you think will happen if you start to get more patients than you can handle?"

"I'll hire an associate," I answered promptly.

"And...?" my uncle prodded.

"And I keep 40 per cent of what he or she bills out," I continued. "That's standard in the industry."

"And eventually...?" Uncle Bill continued.

"I hire perhaps two associates and I can take more time off. There are quite a few optometrists who are either semi-retired or are women who want to devote some of their time to raising their families and don't want to work full-time. In fact, when I went into this profession, I thought it would be ideal for me if I ever got married and had children. I could work part-time and still bring home a good living."

"So, building your practice to the point where you have one or two associates down the line is something for you to shoot for. You could probably earn double or triple what you're making now working for Cyclops, and that doesn't even include your profit on the sale of glasses, contacts and so on. Even if it costs you as much as $250,000 to invest in your business that's a pretty good return on investment."

"$250,000?"

"If we assume $200,000 for equipment as you said, you should allow another $50,000 for leasehold improvements and furniture. You'll also need a bit of working capital to get you through the first couple of months until your patients pay you. What I suggest you do in the next couple of days is put together a business plan. Why don't you visit all three locations that are for sale and get an idea of exactly what you could buy? Then, do some budgeting on the assumption you set up your own shop from scratch. Figure the number of patients you can realistically see each day and how much each one will bring you in revenue. Then you can calculate your potential income over a twelve-month period. From that, you can subtract your salary costs, rent, and so on, and figure out what's left over to pay off debt and provide an income to you."

"I've done some preliminary number-crunching, Uncle Bill. But I suppose I can refine my calculations over the next couple of days."

"I'll be happy to go through the stuff with you but I think you can probably get a pretty good start on your own. After all, you have the advantage of knowing your own profession."

"Do I need to incorporate or anything like that?" I asked.

"Probably not initially," Uncle Bill said. "When you borrow money, the lending institution is going to require your personal guarantee anyhow, so the limited liability protection afforded by setting up a separate legal entity through incorporation really isn't going to matter. But when you start to make big money, which I simply define as more than you need to live, then you should consider incorporating your business."

"Why wait until I'm making big money?"

"There are some major tax advantages to being incorporated once you're profitable," Uncle Bill said. "Since the early '70s, Canada has had a tax structure that favours incorporation for profitable businesses. You see, even at relatively modest income levels, an individual is soon paying tax at 45 to 50 per cent on each dollar of income. But a small incorporated business, which is, again, an entity that is separate from its owners, can earn up to $200,000 a year of business profits and pay only about 20 per cent tax. The $200,000 annual limit has been around for quite a number of years now."

"What does that mean to me?"

"Let's take an easy illustration," Uncle Bill said. "Let's assume your business grows to the point where, within a few years, your profit before you take any salary is $200,000. You've paid your employees and covered all your overhead. Got it so far?"

"Yes," I said. "All the bills are paid, my employees are paid, I haven't been paid, but my profit is $200,000."

"Let's assume you personally need a pre-tax income of $100,000 which leaves you after taxes enough money to pay all your bills, contribute to an RRSP, cover a mutual fund investment program and so on."

"What you're basically saying is the take-home on my $100,000 income should cover all my *living and saving expenses.*"

"Correct," Uncle Bill nodded. "So, you take out $100,000 and have $100,000 left in the business. If you're unincorporated, that second $100,000 gets taxed at your top personal rate, which would be anywhere from 45 to 55 per cent."

"That's between $45,000 and $55,000," I said.

"I don't know which is the bigger crime," Uncle Bill responded, "the way we're taxed or the way the tax dollars have been spent."

"Do tell, Uncle Bill," I commented, then realized something. "Hey, you said the corporate rate is only about 20 per cent. So, if the second $100,000 stays in the business, the taxes would only be $20,000. The corporation would be ahead by about $30,000 on the tax side and because I control the corporation..."

"You would control the disposition of $80,000 after-tax dollars."

"Wonderful," I said. "Why does the government allow this? It's not out of any love for me or concern for my success or financial well-being, I'm sure."

"The government wants small businesses to use cheaply-taxed profits, which I sometimes call eighty-cent dollars—the after 20 per cent tax dollars—for business expansion," Uncle Bill said. "In other words, it provides a way that a small business can finance its growth from within, without borrowing. That means machinery, inventory, staff..."

I was confused again. This was a little tougher learning curve than the simple, straightforward financial planning, get an RRSP, buy mutual funds, stuff. "Uncle Bill, you just got through telling me I'm better off without a lot of machinery or inventory."

"Exactly," he said, "and here's the key point. *If you have a profitable small business that qualifies for the low rate of corporate tax, you can use those eighty-cent after-tax dollars to create investment capital for yourself*. Even though you wouldn't be permitted to draw out the money into your own hands without paying personal tax, the corporation could make investments on your behalf. And where do you think the corporation would invest its money?"

"I don't know," I said sarcastically. "Maybe it should pay fees to you."

"Keep talking that way and I'll charge you combat pay," Uncle Bill said sternly. "Most of the time you're a pleasure, Andrea, but when you're confused you tend to get touchy."

"I'm only joking, Uncle Bill," I said.

He nodded and continued. "Look, you, yourself, have already figured out that a small business is really nothing more than an extension of its owners and you recognize that you could own all the shares in this corporation. So, if you like term-deposits, your company would invest in term-deposits. If you like stocks, your company could play the stock market. If you wanted mutual funds, real estate, gold, silver, even paintings and antiques, your company could buy all this on your behalf. The point is *you* would control the wealth even if you don't own it directly."

"I see," I said as the light went on. "Instead of only having fifty-cent dollars after personal taxes to control and dispose of directly, I would control and be able to indirectly dispose of my company's eighty-cent dollars," I summarized. "Which means I can invest it any way I want. So, if I want to buy more growth mutual funds the company could buy a lot more than I could." I savoured that thought for a moment. "*I can use the system instead of the system using me.* Life is good. Why didn't I go into my own business years ago?"

Uncle Bill didn't bother answering.

"I know," I said, "I just had to be ready and now the time has come."

"You're not doing badly, my dear," he said. "You're just what...30? It's the perfect time for you. Now, there's a lot more to owning your own business than we can cover in one night. After you've got your game plan together, you should probably find an accountant who'll help you get started and assist you in setting up your bookkeeping. I'm afraid I'm a little far removed from all that and besides, with the amount that I like to travel, I won't always be around for you."

"I don't have an accountant," I said. "For the last, umpteen years, you and I have done my taxes right here on your computer and they've been pretty simple. I don't even know any accountants. Any advice on finding one?"

"It's like trying to find any other kind of professional," Uncle Bill said slowly, almost guardedly. "If you don't know where to go, you ask around, speak to your friends, and then go to someone who comes with a high recommendation. It's also important that you feel comfortable....some compatibility with this person... and you can communicate openly and effectively."

"Sounds no different than general principles for shopping around for a doctor or an optometrist," I said.

Uncle Bill nodded. "One bit of concrete advice I can give you, though, is you need to know the type of accountant you're dealing with."

"Ha! Bean counters. Even you've called them bean counters. What more do I need to know?"

"Ah, well, it's not quite that simple," Uncle Bill said. "You see, broadly speaking, accountants in public practice come in two types."

"You sound like you're describing gerbils," I laughed.

"No, they don't use quite as much paper these days," Uncle Bill shot back and we both had a good laugh before he continued. "Some accountants prefer dealing with big business. Like, here in Ottawa, they'd rather work with the big software companies, the electronics firms, and so on. Then there are accountants who prefer working with small businesses."

"Well, that simplifies my search," I said. "I'll look for someone who fits the second category, though I guess I might find that one of the larger firms has a small business unit in its practice."

"It's possible," Uncle Bill nodded, "but I think you're better off dealing with a smaller firm that's a sole proprietorship or has, say, three or four partners at most. Chances are you'll get better treatment from a firm accustomed to dealing with small business clients, that is itself a small business. Small firms would likely value your business more than larger firms and definitely would tend to charge lower fees."

"Basically, you're saying I'd be better off as a small fish in a small pond rather than being a small fish in a big pond."

"That's one way to put it," Uncle Bill said.

"Uncle Bill, I feel so much better now than I did when I came to see you earlier. I'm sure I can develop my own business plan and I'll be a lot better off without having some pompous fool at head office dictating how many patients I should or shouldn't see. I'll get on my exploration of business opportunities first thing in the morning."

"You might have to work harder than you ever did in your life for a short while," Uncle Bill said. "But the rewards will be there for you. Now, relax. You have three business leads to start with, compliments of our good friend, my computer. But don't jump right away. Take your time. A month more or less isn't going to make a lot of difference."

"I'm going to find the opportunity that's best suited to me," I assured him. "And I won't be afraid to use experts. I'll find an accountant I can work with closely and a lawyer who can handle whatever legal work I need."

"Excellent, Andrea." Uncle Bill applauded my approach. "If you want any help from me, I'd be glad to do what I can for you as well. Don't be too proud to ask for help. Friends and family might not always be able to back you with money, but they can often help you out with time and sympathetic ears."

"Uncle Bill," I said feeling a bit overwhelmed. "I read a saying about how you can pick your friends but you can't pick your relatives. I lucked out with you. A relative who's also a true friend!"

"Now, calm down, my dear," Uncle Bill said, dabbing self-consciously at his eye. "You don't want to make an old man cry, do you? And no, I don't want an answer. Anyway, enough heavy stuff for this evening. Would you like to have a game of 3-D Scrabble? We don't even have to move. We can play on the computer."

I nodded my head enthusiastically.

"How about another cup of coffee first?" he added.

"Only if you teach me how to use your newfangled machine."

"It's really quite simple," said Uncle Bill. "Even an optometrist shouldn't have too much trouble with it."

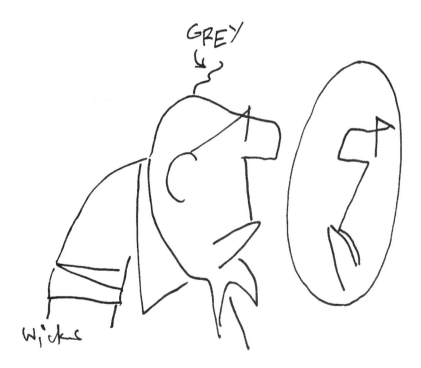

CHAPTER FIFTEEN

DECEMBER 2015
LOGAN'S STORY:
HAPPY BIRTHDAY, UNCLE BILL

THIS MORNING, as I was getting dressed, Colleen came up behind me and plucked the first grey hair out of my head. Kind of fitting, perhaps, that on the occasion of your 65th birthday, Uncle Bill, I should have the first intimation that some day I, too, will be a senior citizen. You've been quite a role model to us and I'm sure we'll still be able to learn from you for many years to come. I thought I should end this—my contribution to your birthday gift—with a short outline of what Colleen and I have been able to accomplish—with no small thanks to you.

First, and most important, we have Sam, who is, at age 15, believe it or not, a well-adjusted teenager. He's been working since September, would you believe, delivering the Times-Herald on a motorized skateboard...quite different from when I was a kid. He's a real budding tycoon because on his fancy new contraption, he can cover a route larger than Andrea and I handled *together* in our day. I don't know how he's going to handle heavy snowstorms yet, but with the new climate-control satellite in place, he may just be in luck.

Then there's Vanessa, age six, pretty as a picture, and all excited about being allowed to attend her Great-Uncle Bill's birthday party. If there's anything I have to thank you for, it's for teaching me to work smart, not hard. I've been able to take the time to enjoy my kids, unlike many other dads.

On the financial side, Colleen and I have done pretty well. That first rental property is now paid for, and it's worth about $150,000. Three months ago, we burned the mortgage on our home and when we had our semi-annual insurance appraisal, it came in at around $250,000. So we've got $400,000 in real estate along with almost $90,000 in RRSPs and other investments. Almost half a million dollars at our age 35—not bad. Our target is for us to be millionaires within the next decade and I have a suspicion we'll beat that goal by at least a couple of years. We're looking at an investment property, a small apartment building with six units. As you know, Colleen loves to fix and decorate, and now that Vanessa's in school, she's got the time.

I'm still working for the same company and it looks like I may become regional manager next year, if I can convince them to let me stay in Ottawa and not move to Regina. Actually, there are times when I find myself starting to think about a change— my own business. So you never know. You were right; not having any mortgage payments gives a person a lot of flexibility. Who knows? If the right opportunity comes along, I may just take the plunge. But you can be sure we'll bounce our ideas off you first! There's plenty of time. You've taught us well. Your concept of getting rich slowly works—for that and for your love, Colleen and I thank you.

CHAPTER SIXTEEN

ANDREA'S STORY:
THE BUSINESS NOW TAKES CARE OF ME

IT'S HARD TO BELIEVE that five years have passed since I took your advice in setting up my own shop. You were right. Those first couple of years, I worked harder than I ever thought I would. But it's paid off and I expect my business is worth a pretty penny. I'm not a real estate tycoon like my brother, but I've taken your advice and diversified and, even if all else fails, God bless RRSPs.

Most of all, Uncle Bill, I'm grateful for the fact you taught me how important it is to lead a balanced life. After two hard years of slugging away at making my business grow, you finally convinced me to take a vacation, and if I hadn't, I wouldn't have met Jim. As you know, we're expecting our first baby next spring—better late than never—and I hope it's a boy so we can name him Bill; Wilhemena just doesn't have the same ring to it.

Believe it or not, we've been giving serious thought to buying a house in time for junior's arrival. After all, a fully paid house is an important cornerstone of financial security! You see, Uncle Bill, I've learned your lessons well and Jim is a pretty good study—although, you know these graphic artist types—I've got my hands full keeping his feet firmly planted on the ground. But we're happy and that's what counts.

I remember what you told Logan and me 20 years ago about how money squabbles are the biggest problem in most marriages. This is one problem we're quite content to live without. It's kind of nice not to have anything to fight about. I'm going to take three months off (at least) when little Bill (?) is born. I've already lined up a replacement to run my practice. We'll be spending a lot of time with you, if that's okay. I'm sure you remember how to change diapers. It's like riding a bicycle—you never forget. Just kidding, Uncle Bill. You make the coffee and I'll deal with the rest...

CHAPTER SEVENTEEN

DECEMBER 6, 2015
LOGAN'S AND ANDREA'S STORY:
GOOD-BYE AND GOOD LUCK

WELL, THERE YOU HAVE IT, the story of Uncle Bill and us and how he advised and guided us on the road to financial independence and security. We hope he'll be with us for a good long time yet, because our kids have a lot to learn and we don't want anything to get lost in translation. If *you* can use any of the information or ideas our Uncle Bill taught us, good for you! Good luck, God bless, and here's to a bright and happy future for all of us.

The Springbank Wealthy Series
Order Now!

How do people with no greater advantages than you manage to achieve so much more success? In his highly-readable books on personal financial planning, Henry Zimmer gives the answers, outlining simple techniques for making your income work harder and helping your investments grow.

THE WEALTHY PROCRASTINATOR
Financial planning for those over forty!

Unlike David Chilton's The Wealthy Barber, Zimmer's new book, The Wealthy Procrastinator is aimed at men and women over forty. This intriguing story spans a twenty-year period from 1995 to 2015, anticipating the kind of political, social and economic restructuring that might occur and its effect on the ordinary Canadian. Using Zimmer's commonsense principles, the book's fictional heroes progress from mid-life financial chaos to a successful retirement . The Wealthy Procrastinator goes beyond the basics of mortgage prepayment, mutual fund programs and life insurance protection to cover such issues as the wise use of severance payments, inheritances, wills, and specific criteria for buying or starting a business.

Now Available

"For people over forty who have neglected their financial planning, The Wealthy Procrastinator takes the mystery out of money management. If you want to spend less time worrying about your financial future and more time enjoying life, I strongly recommend it."

Dian Cohen, former Financial Edior,
CTV News

Quantity_____   **$15.95**

THE MONEY MANAGER FOR CANADIANS
Henry Zimmer's 70,000 best-seller - updated and revised!

Already a stand-by for investment-minded Canadians, The Money Manager is a useful companion book to the Springbank Wealthy Series. In this new edition, Henry Zimmer has updated his popular guide to show that you don't need to be a mathematical genius to survive in an uncertain economy. This complete and easy-to-understand reference book includes simple tables for calculating investment yields, the costs of borrowing money and leasing, life insurance costs and benefits, current mortgage rates and terms, and other financial arrangements.

Now Available

Quantity   **$15.95**

THE WEALTHY PAPER CARRIERS

For the first time—a motivational story on wealth accumulation for young adults!

The Wealthy Paper Carriers is an entertaining and motivational story that shows young adults how to gain more from life than low-paying, low-prestige jobs with no future. Written in the novel form, it tells the story of a brother and sister faced with various life choices over a twenty-year period. Henry Zimmer demonstrates how success is a matter of working intelligently rather than excessively. He shows how to set goals and priorities and suggests a step by step plan to achieve them. For young people—and anyone intimidated by the world of financial planning—The Wealthy Paper Carriers is easy to read and easy to understand. Written in collaboration with students and teachers, it is particularly recommended for educators.

Now Available

Quantity_____   **$15.95**

THE WEALTHY WOMEN

A story of financial planning for women of all ages.

Destined to be a sure-fire best seller, Henry Zimmer's newest financial planning novel is aimed specifically at Canadian women of all ages and circumstances. Written with extensive input from successful women in various fields, The Wealthy Women reviews the standing of women in our changing society, spotlights exciting opportunities, and suggests practical ways of setting and achieving personal success.

Release: Spring, 1994

Quantity_____   **$15.95**

TOTAL NUMBER OF COPIES OF ALL BOOKS

Quantity_____ x $17.07 (GST Included) = $ _____

Name _____
Firm IF APPLICABLE _____
Title IF APPLICABLE _____
Address _____
City _____ Province _____ Postal Code _____
Telephone (   ) _____ Fax (   ) _____

Please mail or Fax your order to:
Springbank Publishing
5425 Elbow Drive S.W. Calgary, Alberta . T2V 1H7
Fax: (403) 640-9138
Telephone (403) 640-9137 for information only

For bulk orders and to arrange Mr. Zimmer's speaking engagements, please contact: Susan Blanchard: (403) 242-9769
Fax: (403) 686-0889

THE WEALTHY PROCRASTINATOR

Financial planning for those over forty!

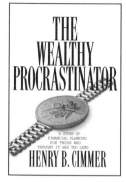

Order Now!

Unlike David Chilton's The Wealthy Barber, Zimmer's new book, The Wealthy Procrastinator is aimed at men and women over forty. This intriguing story spans a twenty-year period from 1995 to 2015, anticipating the kind of political, social and economic restructuring that might occur and its effect on the ordinary Canadian. Using Zimmer's commonsense principles, the book's fictional heroes progress from mid-life financial chaos to a successful retirement . The Wealthy Procrastinator goes beyond the basics of mortgage prepayment, mutual fund programs and life insurance protection to cover such issues as the wise use of severance payments, inheritances, wills, and specific criteria for buying or starting a business.

Now Available

Quantity _____ x $17.07 (GST Included) = $ _____

Name

Firm IF APPLICABLE

Title IF APPLICABLE

Address

City   Province   Postal Code

Telephone ( )   Fax ( )

Please mail or Fax your order to:

Springbank Publishing

5425 Elbow Drive S.W. Calgary, Alberta . T2V 1H7
Fax: 403 640-9138
Telephone 403 640-9137 for information only

For bulk orders and to arrange Mr. Zimmer's speaking engagements, please contact: Susan Blanchard: (403) 242-9769
Fax: (403) 686-0889

THE MONEY MANAGER

Henry Zimmer's 70,000 best-seller - updated and revised!

Order Now!

Already a stand-by for investment-minded Canadians, The Money Manager is a useful companion book to the Springbank Wealthy Series. In this new edition, Henry Zimmer has updated his popular guide to show that you don't need to be a mathematical genius to survive in an uncertain economy. This complete and easy-to-understand reference book includes simple tables for calculating investment yields, the costs of borrowing money and leasing, life insurance costs and benefits, current mortgage rates and terms, and other financial arrangements.

Now Available

Quantity_____ x $17.07 (GST Included) = $_____

Name

Firm IF APPLICABLE

Title IF APPLICABLE

Address

City   Province   Postal Code

Telephone (   )   Fax (   )

Please mail or Fax your order to:

Springbank Publishing

5425 Elbow Drive S.W. Calgary, Alberta . T2V 1H7
Fax: 403 640-9138
Telephone 403 640-9137 for information only

For bulk orders and to arrange Mr. Zimmer's speaking engagements, please contact: Susan Blanchard: (403) 242-9769
Fax: (403) 686-0889